MANAGING FLOAT

IN THE
BANKING INDUSTRY

MANAGING

FLOAT

IN THE
BANKING INDUSTRY

**Opportunities for Earnings
Enhancement through Aggressive
Float Management**

Second Edition

William E. Swords

Probus Publishing Company
Bankers Publishing Company

Library of Congress Number: 91-61956

ISBN 1-55738-317-0

Printed in the United States of America

1 2 3 4 5 6 7 8 9 0

Dedicated to Ronda, Robin,
Sarah and Matthew

Contents

Foreword

Float is a normal part of most payment systems. In the United States, our paper-based payment system creates float at unprecedented levels. Consequently, most large financial institutions have begun addressing the issue of float management.

The purpose of this book is to provide reference material which can be used to educate staff and management on the subject of float and float management.

The opening chapters of this book are devoted to providing users with a thorough understanding of the fundamental concepts of float and float management. From this basis, check collection, workflow management, and other float reduction opportunities are reviewed. A chapter is dedicated to float reporting, outlining various approaches designed to identify opportunities and advertise successes. Float is also addressed from the product manager's perspective. The final chapter provides an overview of the future of float.

Introduction

Float is important. Float must be important to you, or you wouldn't be reading this book. Float is important to financial institutions, or they wouldn't spend millions of dollars to eliminate, reduce, control, track, and manage it. Float is important to the United States government, or Congress would not have directed the Federal Reserve to eliminate or price it in the Monetary Control Act of 1980. And float is important to corporations, creating a demand for such cash management products as lockbox and controlled disbursement.

Float is important because float represents money, and money is important to people. But what is float? Most people have some idea of what float is. Float allows consumers to write checks at the grocery store today against tomorrow's payroll deposit. For bill collectors, float is an excuse — "The check is in the mail." Corporate Cash managers know float as an ally when they pay their bills and as the enemy when they receive funds. To bankers, float is a sizeable portion of the balance sheet that cannot be invested, and is therefore a drag on earnings.

This book will explain contemporary concepts of float and float management, based on the practices of leading U.S. financial institutions. In the interest of simplicity, the term "bank" is used for financial institutions of all types. Although written for bankers, this book also looks at float from the perspectives of check issuing corporations, receivers, the Federal Reserve, and other parties to develop a better understanding of the dynamics of float. Throughout the book, bank float is treated as part of a float cycle that can include several financial institutions as well as businesses and consumers.

Most float in financial institutions represents checks in the process of collection; consequently, much of this book is devoted to managing check float. But other bank activities can generate float as well. Automated Clearing House (ACH) payments usually incur at least one day of float. Delays in processing internal transactions can create float. This book will examine float in non-check areas in order to present a comprehensive approach to float management.

Unlike traditional bank approaches to float, which focused solely on float reduction, this book is based on more recent concepts of float management that view float as a necessary byproduct of a healthy bank operation. No bank ever failed because of a float problem. In fact, an increase in overall float may be the result of an increase in overall business, whereas a sudden and dramatic decrease in float may be a sign of liquidity problems. The only way to eliminate float entirely would be to stop taking deposits — in essence, to stop being a bank.

Modern float management uses a variety of tools, including float allocation, accounting, and pricing, to ensure that unavoidable float does not become an unnecessary burden, while minimizing float within the framework of the bank's business strategies and objectives. This book explains how to use these tools, based on an understanding of float, its sources, its impact on the bank and its role in the payments system.

Float: A Sum of Money

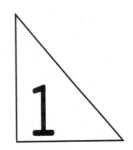

Float Defined

The term **float** means different things to different people. Ambiguities arise not because float is difficult to define, but because float can be viewed from so many different perspectives.

According to *The American Heritage Dictionary*, the word float can be used as either a noun or a verb. As a verb, float is defined: "To cause to remain suspended without sinking or falling." As a noun, float is defined variously as: "Something that floats ... A cork or other floating object on a fishing line ... a hollow ball attached to a lever to regulate the water level in a tank...a soft drink with ice cream floating in it." *The American Heritage Dictionary* also defines float as: "A sum of money representing checks that are outstanding."[1] Webster's New Collegiate Dictionary offers a similar definition of float, along with the usual list of nonfinancial meanings: "An amount of money represented by checks outstanding and in the process of collection."[2]

For the purpose of this book, float is defined as "a sum of money representing checks and other financial instruments that are outstanding and in the process of collection." Although check float accounts for the major portion of this sum, other sources can contribute significantly to overall float. Failure to include float from noncheck sources, including Automated Clearing House (ACH), food coupon, credit card draft, and securities processing, would render an incomplete picture of financial float.

---

1. The American Heritage Dictionary, Boston: Houghton Mifflin Company, 1982, 1985, p. 514.
2. Webster's New Collegiate Dictionary, Springfield: G. & C. Merriam Co., 1980, p. 436.

For the sake of simplicity and clarity, most of the examples and explanations in this book will deal with check float. Most float concepts can be illustrated best within the context of check processing and collection. Many of these concepts can also be applied to noncheck areas. This book will address noncheck areas separately, using concepts developed for the understanding of check float.

The Float Cycle

Understanding float means understanding the float cycle. The **float cycle** is the period of time a check or other financial instrument is outstanding and in the process of collection. Therefore, float represents the sum of money involved in the float cycle.

The float cycle covers every step in the process of collecting a check or financial instrument. It begins with issuance of the item, and it ends with final payment. Over the course of the float cycle, float is shifted from party to party, as the item moves from issuer to receiver, to collecting bank to paying bank.

In the case of a check, the float cycle begins with the issuance of a check, usually as payment for goods or services, or as repayment of debt. As the check is written, it is recorded in the issuer's check register. The bank balance on the issuer's books is reduced, although the actual account balance has not yet been affected. The float cycle will continue while the check is mailed to the payee, handled by the payee, deposited in the payee's bank, processed by the payee's bank, cleared to the issuer's bank, and finally paid against the issuer's account. (See Figure 1.1.)

The float cycle can be short and simple, or it can be long and complex. It may involve as few as two parties, or it may involve many. When an individual writes a check for cash and cashes it at his or her own bank, the float cycle is too short to be measured in days. In this example, two parties are involved, and the issuance, processing, and payment of the check all occur on the same day.

Most float cycles are longer, more complex, and involve several parties. When an individual pays a bill by check and mails the payment, the float cycle can stretch out over several days. Recently, I paid an out-of-state credit card bill with a

Figure 1.1   The Float Cycle

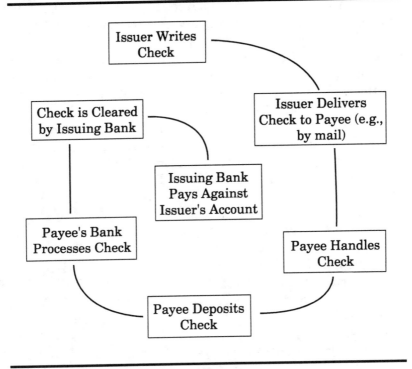

check. My check was outstanding for thirteen days. One day was spent mailing the check, because the check was issued and recorded in my check register on the first of the month but was not mailed or postmarked until the second. The check was in the mail for five days and required two days processing before it was deposited in a commercial bank. The commercial banking system required two business days (in this case four calendar days) to clear the checks, with the item going through two commercial banks and the Federal Reserve Bank prior to final payment of the check on the thirteenth of the month. This example included seven parties: the issuer of the check, the bank on which the check was drawn, the U.S. Postal Service, the credit card company, the depositary bank, a check clearing agent, and the Federal Reserve Bank. The post office was the only party that did not have a financial interest in this float cycle. All other parties had a financial interest in this bill payment, because the cash balances of each were affected at some time during the float cycle.

The number of days in a float cycle can be determined by comparing the date of issue on a check to the date of payment on the check or the checking account statement. In the first case of a check cashed by the issuer at his or her own bank, the date of issue and payment are the same. There were two parties, and no float was created or carried in this float cycle. In the case of my credit card bill payment, the date of issue was the first of the month, and the date of payment was the thirteenth of the month. There were six parties with a monetary interest in this float cycle and twelve days total float.

It is important to note that in our second example only one of the parties, the party who issued the check, incurred the full twelve days of float. All other parties, while taking a monetary interest in this float cycle, incurred less than twelve days float. The credit card company experienced eleven days of float, from the date the check was mailed on the second to receipt of collected funds on the thirteenth. The depositary bank incurred four days of float, from the date of deposit on the ninth to the date of collected funds, again the thirteenth. The check clearing bank and the Federal Reserve Bank each incurred one day of float.

It is also important to note that while I was quite happy with the twelve days of float between the date of issue and the date of payment of my check, the credit card company was probable unhappy with the six days of float it incurred. In my case, I enjoyed the use of the money for twelve days after I wrote my check. In the credit card company's case, they received money six days after posting my payment.

Float Perspectives

Sometimes float and the float cycle can be difficult to understand. Ambiguities arise around the meaning of float not because float itself is hard to define, but because there are so many perspectives from which float, or the float cycle, can be viewed. One's ability to understand float depends on the ability to define and understand one's perspective within the float cycle.

Generally speaking, float can be viewed from three perspectives:

- The issuer's perspective.

- The recipient's perspective.

- The financial intermediary or bank's perspective.

The following section examines check float from each of these perspectives, providing a historical float overview, and describing bank services developed to facilitate cash management and capitalize on the float cycle.

The Check Issuer's Perspective

The check issuer's perspective of float, also known as **disbursement float**, is probably the easiest to understand. The check issuer's perspective encompasses the complete float cycle, whereas float associated with other perspectives represents only part of the cycle. Check issuer float begins with the issuance of the check and ends with payment of the check. Disbursement float represents outstanding checks, and it can be measured by the difference between the check issuer's record of its checking account balance and the account balance on the bank's records.

Almost everyone is familiar with check issuer float. Most bank customers have been in the situation where their checking account statement says their balance is greater than the balance in their checkbook. Most also know that if they use that bank's balance, without accounting for outstanding checks, they are likely to overdraw the account. Customers are aware of float, but most are content to leave these larger balances in their checking accounts.

For a long time, businesses were indifferent to disbursement float. This indifference was based on a lack of appreciation for the amounts involved and on a lack of lucrative investment alternatives. In today's environment, higher short-term interest rates and improved short-term investment alternatives have changed the dynamics of cash management and have piqued business interest in capitalizing on the float cycle.

The treasury departments of large companies routinely invested excess cash balances. Historically, excess balances were determined from the companies' books, not the bank's books, and they were invested for periods of one month or longer. When short term interest rates began to rise in the late 1960s, large corporations began to assign staff with the responsibility of monitoring daily bank balances and investing excess cash for periods of between one day and two weeks. This was the beginning of corporate cash management as we know it today.

Cash managers soon learned that the difference between their companies' records regarding cash balances and the actual cash balances in the bank could be substantial. Corporations began focusing on ways to benefit from the float cycle. Commercial banks were quick to assist cash managers in their quest to better manage corporate cash balances. Banks began offering improved balance reporting services so cash managers could monitor accounts on a daily basis and invest excess balances.

Cash managers also began devising ways to lengthen the float cycle by delaying check clearing. Some companies began using the wrong ZIP code, or no ZIP code, when paying bills by mail. Some cash managers would mail checks to their suppliers corporate headquarters instead of the accounts payable department, hoping to gain float by increasing internal processing time. These efforts were generally successful, because most suppliers used the postmark date of the payment to determine whether payment was timely.

Commercial banks developed **controlled disbursement** accounts to provide cash managers with accurate information on daily check clearings prior to the close of financial markets. With controlled disbursement, cash managers could know the total amount of checks to be posted each day, and they could therefore fund only those items paid and invest the rest. Banks were able to offer controlled disbursement by having corporate customers draw checks on accounts at separate banks with predictable schedules for early receipt of incoming checks. These were typically smaller banks, located outside of Federal Reserve cities, owned by the lead cash management banks or their holding companies.

Once cash managers began writing checks on separate banks for controlled disbursement, the next step was to write checks on banks in remote locations to lengthen the float cycle. This practice, known as **remote disbursement**, has the reporting advantages of controlled disbursement, plus the added feature of increasing the number of days required to clear checks. Remote disbursement takes advantage of the delays inherent in transporting checks to banks in geographically remote or sparsely populated areas, as well as gaps in Federal Reserve and correspondent bank check clearing schedules.

In general, controlled disbursement is an information product that allows cash managers to take advantage of the float that exists in the check clearing process. The purpose of remote disbursement is to actually increase the duration of the float cycle.

Some feel banks and corporate cash managers have gone too far in their efforts to benefit from disbursement float with remote disbursement. Through much of the 1980s, the Federal Reserve has attacked remote disbursement schemes by accelerating check clearing to targeted banks, especially through its High-Dollar Group Sort (HDGS) program. But the companies that benefitted from investing excess balances have been pleased with the improved earnings that have resulted from these efforts. Businesses were not the only ones to benefit from disbursement float. Individuals with high levels of disbursement float have moved money into money market type accounts that allow check writing privileges. In the future, I believe we will continue to see both individuals and businesses seek maximum benefit from disbursement float. In fact, the loss of float is one the factors often cited as an impediment to more widespread use of electronic funds transfer for bill payments.

The Check Recipient's Perspective

Payee float, float from the check recipient's perspective, is float associated with converting a check (a claim to money) into money. The check recipient's float cycle is a subset of the complete float cycle. It begins when the check is given or mailed to the recipient and ends with the receipt of money. From the recipient's perspective, the receipt of money is not merely the credit of funds to a bank account, but the ability to withdraw or invest those funds. If withdrawal or investment of funds is restricted for a period of time after deposit, as is often the case, the float cycle does not end until the funds are freed.

Measuring "recipient float" can be difficult, as the cycle starts when the check is mailed or issued, and the date money is received as investable or collected balances is often not the date of deposit. Nearly everyone is familiar with recipient float. Any delay in converting a check to money is recipient float. Someone who overdraws their account while carrying around a check that could have been deposited to cover the withdrawal is paying dearly for recipient float. Faster conversion of the check into money would have averted a costly and embarrassing bounced check.

For businesses and individuals alike, the incentive to minimize recipient float is based on the desire to obtain money sooner. As with check issuer float, higher interest rates have changed the dynamics of managing recipient float. Recipient float for businesses is normally associated with incoming bill payments and sales receipts. The minimization of recipient float is accomplished in three primary ways:

- Obtaining checks earlier, thereby concluding the float cycle earlier.
- Processing and depositing checks faster.
- Clearing checks faster.

Corporate cash managers now use remittance processing services, commonly known as lockboxes, offered by commercial banks to minimize mail float, processing float, and check collection float associated with payment processing.

Remittance processing services reduce mail float by using unique ZIP codes and post office boxes, with frequent mail pick-up from the post office throughout the early morning. Processing float is minimized by the use of a streamlined, multi-shift processing environment. Lockboxes are generally designed to process the check for immediate deposit, replacing the item with a photocopy that is returned with accompanying remittance documents to the company for posting to accounts receivable records. Check collection float is reduced because the check is deposited early in the processing day, and it is therefore able to meet earlier deadlines for check clearing and presentment.

Reducing float associated with sales receipts is different from reducing float associated with mailed payments. The primary difference is that sales receipts usually are not received centrally, but at geographically dispersed points-of-sale. The cash manager's efforts must focus on collecting checks and cash from each location, balancing receipts, preparing bank deposit, presenting deposits for collection, and consolidating funds deposited in various accounts, often at different banks, into a single account for efficient management. Commercial banks offer a variety of deposit and cash concentration services designed to assist in the collection and consolidation of large volumes of sales receipts.

Whether managing the receipt of payments or sales receipts, the goal of the corporate cash manager is to obtain checks as soon as possible and to convert these checks into collected funds as quickly as possible. Efforts to reduce payee float are designed to minimize the opportunity cost of not investing funds while waiting to receive payments and convert them to money.

The Bank's Perspective

One of the primary functions of our banking system is the collection and payment of checks and other financial instruments. In this role as financial intermediary, banks are key participants in the float cycle. **Bank float** represents a subset of the complete float cycle. It begins with the posting of a deposit containing checks and concludes with the final payment of those checks.

Banks participate in the float cycle in a number of roles, including:

- *Depositary Bank:* The first financial institution to receive a deposited check as it enters the banking system, sometimes referred to as the "bank of first deposit."

- *Check Clearing Intermediary:* A bank that clears checks for other banks.

- *Paying Bank:* The bank on which the check is drawn, and which must make payment for the check when it is presented.

Bank float is measured differently for depositary banks and check clearing banks than for paying banks. In the role of paying bank, bank float is the difference between the dollar amount of items presented for payment and the dollar amount withdrawn from customers' accounts. In a perfect world, a paying bank would incur no paying bank float. In the real world, paying bank float represents checks that the bank has paid for, but for which it has not been paid by its customers. Examples of paying bank float include checks than cannot be debited from customers' accounts due to insufficient funds, stop payments, and invalid account numbers.

The vast majority of bank float is incurred by depositary and check clearing intermediary banks. In these roles, float begins with the acceptance and posting of deposits containing transit checks—checks drawn on other banks. The float cycle ends with receipt of investable funds. Bank float measures the dollar amount of items "in the process of collection." Measuring bank float can be difficult, because of the complexity of determining the date of payment by subsequent clearing intermediaries and the paying bank.

The Federal Reserve System has a unique perspective on bank float. As the largest check clearing intermediary, it participates in the float cycle for over one-third of all checks written in the United States. Unlike other banks, however, the Federal Reserve does not account for float from the date checks are deposited for collection. Instead, the Federal Reserve defers posting of check deposits until the date it anticipates settlement with the paying bank. If all checks are presented to paying banks and paid without delay, the Federal Reserve System records no float. **Federal Reserve float**, or Fed float, therefore represents checks that are not cleared according to the Federal Reserve Banks' published schedules. The bank that deposited the checks gets credit for investable funds in its reserve account, even though the Federal Reserve System has not been paid. Fed float is created as a result of operating inefficiencies, transportation delays, or overly optimistic published availability schedules.

The Monetary Control Act of 1980 directed that the Federal Reserve eliminate Fed float or include it in its pricing of check services. As a result, Fed float has fallen dramatically from an average of $6.5 billion in January 1979 to 566 million for August 1989.

Historically, banks were not particularly concerned with bank float. Float was viewed as an unavoidable cost of doing business. Because most businesses managed funds from their own records without taking advantage of disbursement float, companies generally maintained large excess balances in their bank accounts. These balances were usually more than sufficient to cover bank float associated with an account's deposits. As with check issuers and receivers, however, higher short-term interest rates led banks to focus attention on float. In response, banks assigned staff to find ways of reducing the cost of float. The discipline of float management has grown over the years to become a vital function at nearly all banks.

Today, there are two major components of float management in financial institutions:

1. *Float Reduction:* Efforts to speed the conversion of checks and other financial instruments into money.

2. *Float Allocation:* Efforts to associate float with the depository products and customers that generate it, reducing the portion of customer balances that can be withdrawn or invested, earn interest or earn credits against bank fees. Allocated float is usually labeled "uncollected funds."

Float reduction and float allocation will be discussed in greater detail in subsequent chapters.

Float Perspectives Summarized

Working capital is an essential element of business familiar to most. Float represents working capital associated with the payment process. Float is viewed as a use of working capital by check recipients and financial intermediaries, and it carries an associated opportunity cost. For the check issuer, however, float is a source, not a use, of working capital.

Types of Float

Like any other field, float management has its own specialized vocabulary. While this book contains a complete glossary of float terminology, this section lists definitions for various types of float. Familiarity with the different types of float will make it easier to understand the concepts of float management discussed in later chapters.

Allocated Float: Bank Float identified and associated with a customer or internal department of the bank. Allocated Float is the sum of Customer Float and Internal Bank Float allocated to specific bank units or departments. Allocated Float is often expressed as a percentage of total Bank Float. If Allocated Float exceeds total Bank Float, float allocation is greater than 100 percent.

Bank Float: A sum of money, recorded on the financial books of a bank, representing checks and other financial instruments that are outstanding and are in the process of collection.

Booked Float: A sum of money, representing checks and other financial instruments that are outstanding and in the process of collection, that has been recorded on the financial books of a bank, company, or individual.

Check Float: A sum of money representing checks that are outstanding and in the process of collection.

Collection Float: Float representing checks and other financial instruments deposited in a bank for collection, for which the depositor has not received full availability of funds. Also called Deposit Float.

Customer Float: Bank Float allocated to specific customers, reducing account balances available for withdrawal, investment, or earnings credit against bank fees. Customer Float is allocated to the accounts of customers depositing items for collection. Customer Float allocated in excess of actual Bank Float incurred on customer deposits is called Negative Float or Reverse Float. Customer Float is also referred to as **Priced Float**.

Deposit Float: See Collection Float.

Federal Reserve Float: Funds the Federal Reserve System has credited to a bank's reserve account for checks deposited for collection, but for which the Federal Reserve has not received funds from the paying bank. The Federal Reserve System credits deposits on a deferred basis, according to its published availability schedule, so Federal Reserve Float represents checks not cleared within that schedule. This is in contrast to commercial bank practice, which is to credit deposits immediately, but allocate float to the depositor's account. Therefore, Federal Reserve Float is analogous to Positive Float at a commercial bank. Federal Reserve Float is often referred to as Fed Float.

Float: A sum of money representing checks and other financial instruments that are outstanding and in the process of collection.

Internal Bank Float: Float a bank incurs in its role as a check issuer or a check recipient.

Mail Float: A component of the float cycle. A sum of money representing checks and other financial instruments that are outstanding in the process of delivery to the payee by the postal system or other carrier. Mail float covers the period of time beginning when the issuer releases the item to a carrier and ending when the item is delivered to the payee or its agent (e.g., its lockbox bank).

Negative Float: A sum of money representing Customer Float allocated in excess of actual Bank Float incurred on those customers' deposits. Negative Float represents monies received by the bank for deposited items that have not been made available to customers. Negative Float is generally considered a source of revenue for banks. Negative Float is also referred to as Reverse Float.

Noncheck Float: A sum of money representing financial instruments other than checks that are outstanding and in the process of collection.

Positive Float: A sum of money representing the difference between Bank Float and Customer Float when a bank incurs more float on customers' deposits than it allocates as Customer Float. Positive Float represents monies that have been made available to depositing customers but that have not been collected by the bank. Positive Float is generally considered a reduction of revenue for banks.

Priced Float: See Customer Float.

Processing Float: A component of the float cycle. A sum of money representing checks and other financial instruments in the float cycle while under the physical control of a participant in that cycle. For example, a check recipient can incur processing float while posting payments to accounts receivable, preparing bank deposits, or delivering deposits to a bank. A bank can incur processing float while encoding and sorting checks, handling rejected items, balancing, and preparing cash letters.

Receiving Float: A sum of money representing checks and other financial instruments received as payments or receipts, that are in the process of collection and conversion to money.

Reverse Float: See Negative Float.

Unallocated Float: Any Bank Float not allocated to customers or internal bank units.

Unbooked Float: A sum of money representing checks and other financial instruments received by a bank, individual, or corporation that are outstanding and in the process of collection, but that have not been recorded on the financial books of that entity.

Float
Management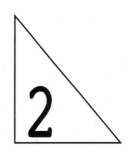

The Role of Float Management

Float management is an important aspect of overall bank management. The purpose of float management is to help establish and maintain strong bank earnings. Effective float management improves earnings, while poor float management depresses earnings.

Traditionally, float managers have pursued the goal of improved earnings through float reduction and float allocation. The aim of float reduction is to shorten the float cycle by accelerating check collection, improving workflow, streamlining processing, and otherwise cutting the time it takes to turn checks and other items into money. Float allocation gives banks a way to recoup the cost of float by assigning it to the depositors, products, and internal departments that create it. The bank can then withhold availability of uncollected funds, reduce interest payments accordingly, take account of float in determining bank compensation for services, or include the cost of float in bank pricing.

The float manager must maintain a proper balance in float reduction and float allocation efforts. When a customer deposits checks drawn on other financial institutions, the bank must collect the checks before usable funds are obtained. Generally, faster check collections contributes to improved earnings.

Likewise, if depositing customers withdraw funds before their checks are collected, earnings can be reduced because the bank has given the customer money that the bank has not collected. If, however, customers are denied reasonable access to deposited funds, earnings can also be hurt because customers unhappy with the bank's service might leave the bank. The float managers' ability to improve earnings is in part based on his or her ability to establish the proper balance between check collection efforts and customer funds availability issues.

In addition to float reduction and float allocation, float management is often charged with two other important responsibilities. One is ensuring that float is categorized and accounted for accurately and advantageously. Seemingly insignificant differences in the way float is categorized on the bank's books can have a noticeable impact on a bank's reported Return on Assets and Return on Equity. In the tough competitive environment most banks face today, even a small improvement in performance ratios can give a bank an edge in capital markets and the mergers and acquisitions arena.

Another vital function of float management is float reporting. Although float is usually accounted for in standard financial reports, the information is buried. Float reporting focuses on the type of information needed to understand float within the bank and to support informed decision making about how to manage it. Float reporting also provides a way to monitor the success of float management activities and to make adjustments as appropriate.

Float and the Balance Sheet

Banking is based on a pooling concept. Pools of liabilities are attracted from depositors to fund pools of assets, such as loans and investments. No one knows specifically how one's money is being used by a bank, even though we do know how a bank uses its deposits in total. Effective bank management requires an understanding of the inter-relationships between asset pools and liability pools (see Table 2.1).

The amount of money a bank can afford to spend on attracting deposit dollars is based on the amount of money that the bank can expect to earn on those deposits. The cost of attracting deposits and the anticipated revenue opportunities associated with these deposits must be considered. The costs associated with attracting pools of deposits include interest expense, operating expense, and overhead expense. The revenue associated with attracting pools of deposits include fee income and interest income on the investment of deposited funds.

Table 2.1   Float National Bank

Balance Sheet in Millions

Assets		*Liabilities and Capital*	
Cash Due-From	$ 150	Demand Deposits	$ 350
Investments	$ 250	Time Deposits	$ 450
Loans	$ 530	Certificate of Deposits	$ 110
Fixed Assets	$ 60	Other Liabilities	$ 20
Other Assets	$ 10	Capital	$ 70
Total Assets	$1,000	Total Liabilities & Capital	$1,000

Unfortunately, a bank cannot earn interest income on its total deposits. Interest is only earned on the investable portion of a bank's funds. A portion of a bank's deposits, liabilities, and capital are needed to support nonearning assets— assets that do not accrue interest.

Nonearning assets include such items as buildings, equipment, and other fixed assets needed to conduct the business of banking. Past-due loans that are no longer accruing interest and repossessed property form another category of nonearning assets.

The category Cash Due-From represents also sterile or noninterest earning assets associated with attracting and retaining deposits. The following general asset classifications are found in Cash Due-From:

- **Vault Cash:** Coin and Currency in bank vaults

- **Federal Reserve Account:** Collected deposits with the Federal Reserve Bank

- **Due-From Balances:** Deposits with other financial institutions.

- **Cash Items** in the Process of Collection (CIPC).

- **Suspense:** Items suspended in the process of collection, often requiring research or other handling prior to resolution.

The float manager contributes to earnings by maximizing the investable portion of a bank's total deposits. This is accomplished by collecting checks in a prompt and cost effective manner (i.e., float reduction) and by controlling or managing customers' access to deposited funds (i.e., float allocation). Float management cannot simply focus on reducing Cash Due-From balances. Effective float management must also focus on how depository products are structured and priced.

Float Reduction

Float reduction efforts improve earnings because float reduction increases investable funds, thus allowing a bank to hold an interest earning asset instead of float, a sterile asset.

Banks reduce float by collecting checks and other items faster. Float reduction occurs when checks that would have been collected in two days are collected in one day, or when checks that would have been collected in one day are collected the same day. Improved check collection can be accomplished by reducing the time associated with handling and processing items, or by choosing check clearing agents that offer better availability or deadlines.

Often, reducing float requires both. For example, a bank that takes two days to collect checks drawn on banks in a particular city might be able to reduce its clearing time to one day by using an alternative clearing agent. If, however, the new clearing agent has an earlier deposit deadline than the current agent, the bank would have to reduce processing time to have checks ready in time. Failure to speed up check processing could reduce or eliminate the benefit of selecting the new clearing agent. In later chapters, we will explore ways of reducing float in much greater detail. But before proceeding, it is important to learn how to quantify the value of float reduction.

Quantifying the benefits of float reduction is important for several reasons. The first reason is that not all float reduction opportunities are worth pursuing. There is almost always a cost of reducing float. Clearing agents charge fees for their services. If a clearing agent is in another city, there is a cost for transporting checks. Expedited check processing might increase operating costs. The value of a reduction in float might not justify the cost.

Secondly, quantification also helps prioritize float reduction opportunities. A bank can only pursue a limited number of projects at a time. Those with the greatest expected benefit are usually handled first. Float projects must compete for resources and management attention, not only with other float projects, but also with new product launches, customer service programs, productivity improvements, and other initiatives. In fact, some competing projects could be mutually exclusive. For instance, plans to reduce float by cutting processing time for proof encoding might conflict with proposed staff cuts in the proof department. Quantifying the benefit of float reduction allows informed decision making.

Third, quantifying float reduction opportunities both before and after implementation is an excellent way to gauge the effectiveness of float reduction efforts. Failure to achieve the full value of expected float reduction benefits might indicate the need for changes in the original plan, or might point out weakness in the original analysis.

Quantifying the value of float reduction efforts is a function of the following:

- The amount of float reduction.
- Its impact on Required Reserves.
- The opportunity investment rate.
- Change in operating expense or clearing costs.

The amount of float reduction is simply the value of funds that will be collected sooner, multiplied by the number of days saved. If $1 million of checks are cleared two days faster, the float reduction would be $2 million:

$$\$1,000,000 \times 2 \text{ days} = \$2,000,000 \text{ float reduction}$$

A reduction in check float results in a decrease in one of the Cash Due-From accounts—Cash Items in the Process of Collection (CIPC). But a reduction in check float also increases a bank's Required Reserves. Required Reserves are funds that financial institutions must by law maintain in

Vault Cash or in Federal Reserve Bank accounts to ensure liquidity to pay depositors claims. Required Reserves are equal to a fraction of transaction account and certain other deposit liabilities. Because CIPC is deducted from deposits before calculating the reserve requirement, a reduction in float increases the deposit base for Required Reserves. The net result is that a reduction in check float is partially offset by increases in other Cash and Due-From accounts. This increase in nonearning assets must be deducted from the amount of float reduced when quantifying the value of float reduction.

The **opportunity investment rate** is the rate of interest the bank can expect to receive when it invests the increase in available funds in earning assets. This rate is multiplied by the net reduction in float, after adjusting for Required Reserves, to determine the increase in interest income expected from float reduction.

In the short term, most float improvements either reduce borrowing or increase sales of Fed Funds. Fed Funds are sums lent among banks, overnight or for terms of up to 30 days, to adjust their balances in Federal Reserve Bank accounts to meet required reserves. Float benefits are often quantified using the projected average Fed Funds rate.

If float reductions are long term or permanent, however, it may be more appropriate to use a different rate than the Fed Funds rate. A long-term increase in investable funds could be used to make loans, which generally yield more than Fed Funds, or reduce the need for high-priced deposits. Banks often use a pooled cost-of-funds, which blends the rates paid on various deposits and liabilities, to value float reductions.

Determination of the opportunity investment rate is frequently controversial. A good rule of thumb is to let someone else choose the rate. An appropriate earnings rate should approximate the actual earnings the bank expects to earn from similar sources of funds. Normally the bank's financial department can choose an appropriate rate, and normally this rate will approximate the current Fed Funds rate.

Finally, the expenses associated with float reduction are deducted from the increase in interest income to determine the net improvement in earnings resulting from a reduction in float.

The formula for this calculation is:

$$FR - R = F \times IR = I - E = B$$

Amount of Float Reduction (FR) – Increase in Required Reserves (R) = Net Increase in Investable Funds (F) x Opportunity Investment Rate (IR) = Increase in Interest Income (I) – Expenses for Float Reduction (E) = Benefit of Float Reduction (B)

Let us consider an example. A float manager can collect a daily average of $100,000 in checks one day sooner by switching to a new clearing agent. The prospective clearing agent is located out-of-state, requiring courier delivery of checks at an annual cost of $2,500. The new clearing agent also charges more for check clearing than the current agent, totalling $900 a year in additional fees. In this example there is no increase in processing costs. The benefit of float reduction is calculated in Table 2.2.

Table 2.2   Sample Analysis of Float Reduction Efforts

Average daily float reduction	$100,000
Less reserve requirement impact	(12,000)
Net new investable funds	$ 88,000
Opportunity investment rate	10%
Annual increase in interest income	$ 8,000
Less increase in annual costs:	
Courier expense	$2,500
Clearing fees	900
Total new annual costs	(3,400)
Net Annual Float Reduction Benefit	$ 5,400

It is important to note several important factors when performing a float benefit analysis. Care should be taken to assure that the float benefit occurs every day. For example, sometimes items that are cleared in two days Monday through Thursday may be cleared in one business day on Fridays. If the float manager discovers a way to collect these items in one day every day, the actual float reduction benefit will only occur on four out of seven calendar days. If this were the case in Table 2.2, the reduction in float would be reduced by $42,857 ($100,000 X 3/7), and benefits would be reduced by $3,771.

Float reduction benefits should also be discounted to account for anticipated transportation delays and missed deadlines. If past courier performance for similar transportation has resulted in transportation-related deadline misses of 5 percent (i.e., one miss in every twenty days) the float reduction amount should be reduced by 5 percent. In the previous example, the float reduction amount would be reduced by $5,000, and our annual increase in interest income would be reduced $400.

All float changes, both increases and decreases, should be quantified net of Required Reserves. In the previous example, we have assumed no change to our bank's total deposits or to our bank's total liabilities. Our float reduction efforts have simply moved dollars from float, a sterile asset, into an earning asset by collecting checks one day faster. Implied in this example is that our depositing customers have not changed withdrawal patterns as a result of the float manager's improved check collection efforts. Our float manager's effort to collect checks faster has, therefore, increased net reservable deposits, as explained earlier.

Float reduction efforts, particularly those that yield marginal benefits, should be reviewed periodically to assure continued practicality. Operating costs and clearing fees have a way of increasing over time, interest rates change, and the number and dollar volume of items that are being cleared faster can also change. Sometimes a float reduction effort that saved money last year can cost money this year and should be discontinued.

Float Allocation

Float allocation improves earnings because float allocation tends to increase a bank's investable funds by influencing the length time a customer will leave deposited funds in the bank. Banks increase float allocation when deposits that were once assigned one day float are assigned two days float, or when deposits that were once assigned no float are assigned one day float.

The length of time that a customer leaves deposited funds in the bank is measured by the "length of stay." Banks attempt to influence a customer's length of stay by differentiating between ledger balances and collected balances. Both length of stay and ledger versus collected balances are important concepts for the float manager to understand.

Length of Stay

When customers deposit checks into their accounts, the bank performs three basic services:

- The check or checks are collected, converted from a claim to money into money.

- The funds are maintained in a safe place.

- The bank facilitates the transfer of payments between the depositing customer and others, usually by check or electronic funds transfer.

The length of time deposited funds remain on deposit is commonly called **length of stay** and represents the average number of days between when a customer makes a deposit and when funds are paid out. The length of stay is calculated by dividing the average daily balance by the average daily deposit amount.

$$\frac{\text{Average Daily Balance}}{\text{Average Daily Deposit}} = \text{Length of Stay}$$

Historically, the length of stay for all bank depositors was several days. For most personal accounts, the length of stay remains rather large, often averaging seven days or more.

For example, a customer that made $1,800 in deposits during a 30-day month and maintained an average balance of $300 would have a 5-day length of stay. The length of stay is computed by dividing the $300 average daily balance by the $60 average daily deposit ($1,800 in total deposits divided by 30 calendar days equals $60). It is important to note that the length of stay is not affected by the actual number of deposits that the customer makes during the period, only by the average daily deposit amount.

Ledger Balances versus Collected Balances

Float allocation is the tool that allows a bank to differentiate between ledger balances and collected balances. The **ledger balance** is the sum of money that represents the bank's record of deposit account balances after the posting of all debits and credits. The ledger balance is the account balance reported for accounting purposes, and the balance reported on checking account statements. The **collected balance** is the sum of money that represents the deposit account balances in excess of any float allocated to the account. Stated another way, the collected balance is the ledger balance less uncollected funds or float. The collected balance is the bank's approximation of monies on deposit for which the bank has received investable funds for deposited items.

Understanding collected balances at the bank level is fairly simple. At the bank level, collected balances equal total deposits less float. Conceptually, understanding collected balances at the customer level is just as simple; namely, collected balances are total customer balances less float. In practice, however, identifying any given customer's appropriate level of float can be quite complex. The ability to determine collected balances at the customer level is important for bank profitability, because banks attempt to influence customer behavior by differentiating between ledger balances and collected balances at the customer level.

For years, banks have been prohibited from paying interest on the demand deposit accounts of business and corporate customers. But instead of paying interest, banks have allowed business customers to use account balances to offset service changes or fees for banking related services. This practice, known as account analysis, values balances held in compensation for bank services according to an earnings credit rate. If a customer does not maintain sufficient compensating balances to pay for services provided, the customer is asked to increase balances accordingly or pay explicit service charges or banks fees.

Table 2.3 is a typical monthly account analysis statement for a corporate customer. The statement shows the average ledger balance, average uncollected funds, the resulting average collected balance, the rate used to calculate the earnings credit, and the amount of earnings credit for collected balances. It also includes a detailed listing of fees for bank services, and a calculation of whether the earnings credit is

Table 2.3   Account Analysis

January 1991

XYZ Corporation   **Account Number: 111-22-333-4**

Balance Summary:

Average Ledger Balance	$100,000
Average Uncollected Funds	− 30,000
Average Collected Balance	= 70,000
Annual Earning Credit Rate	6.5%
Earnings Credit	$386.44

Itemized Services:

Account Maintenance		$15.00
Checks Paid	623 @ .15	93.45
Deposits	21 @ .30	6.30
Deposited Checks	1,130 @ .12	135.60
Wire Transfers	8 @ $10	80.00
Total Services		$330.35

Compensating Balance Calculation:

Average Collected Balances Held	$70,000
Collected Balances Required for Itemized Services	
(at 6.5% Earnings Credit Rate)	− 59,840
Collected Balance Surplus/(Deficit)	= $10,160

sufficient to cover total fees. The excess or deficiency is then converted to a collected balance equivalent, which shows the increase or decrease in collected balances that would have made the earnings credit equal fees for the period.

Initially, banks used ledger balances to determine whether a customer was providing adequate compensation for bank services. Collected balances were not used because of the difficulty in obtaining the float data at the customer level, and because customers tended to maintain large excess balances; that is, balances well in excess of the level required to pay for services rendered.

Once businesses began employing cash management techniques, however, banks discovered a real need to differentiate between ledger balances and collected balances at the customer level. The importance of using the collected balance, rather that the ledger balance in determining the value of a customer's account, can be seen in the following example.

Three customers each use the same level of services and each maintain $100,000 in ledger balances. But there is one important difference between customers: customer A maintains a 5-day length of stay, customer B maintains a 2-day length of stay, and customer C maintains a 1-day length of stay. If we assume a 30-day month, this means customer A deposited $600,000, customer B deposited $1,500,000, and customer C deposited $3,000,000 during the month. Each deposit required an average of 1.5 days to collect. Table 2.4 shows the resulting impact on collected balances.

Table 2.4   Length of Stay and Collected Balances

	A	B	C
Total monthly deposits	$600,000	$1,500,000	$3,000,000
Total float	$900,000	$2,500,000	$4,500,000
Length of stay	5 days	2 days	1 day
Average ledger balance	$100,000	$100,000	$100,000
Average daily float	$30,000	$75,000	$150,000
Average collected balance	$70,000	$25,000	$(50,000)

Table 2.4 points out the importance of using the collected balance, rather than the ledger balance, in determining the relative profitability of a customer, and it shows the related impact of a change in the length of stay ratio.

Today, most banks differentiate between ledger balances and collected balances for business accounts by employing account analysis. Some banks differentiate between ledger balances and collected balances for interest bearing accounts. Most banks, however, do not differentiate between ledger balance and collected balance for the bulk of personal accounts. This unwillingness to identify float at the personal account level occurs because the difference between ledger and collected is normally small, implying a longer length of stay than most business accounts, and because the service charges for most individual accounts are not as directly related to balance levels as are business accounts.

Float Allocation Benefits

Float allocation will improve earnings when float allocation influences how customers manage the flow of funds through their accounts. Most of the benefits associated with float allocation are realized through account analysis. Even within the group of analyzed accounts, different types of customers will react differently to a change in float allocations. Most analyzed accounts will react to changes in customer availability. This occurs because most business customers consciously manage account balances held to compensate banks for services received. Customers who actively manage compensating balances normally fall into three general categories:

1. Some business customers choose to pay for services through compensating balances. These customers try to maintain collected balances close to the level required to pay for services, so an increase in allocated float will cause them to leave more funds in their accounts to provide adequate compensation.

2. Some business customers choose to pay all or part of their bills in the form of fees. These customers usually try to maintain minimal collected balances in their accounts, so a change in allocated float will limit their ability to withdraw funds.

3. Some business customers choose to overpay a bank for services, usually in hopes of gaining favored customer status. For these customers, an increase in allocated float will cause them to leave more funds in their accounts to overpay the bank.

Only those customers whose deposit and withdrawal patterns are completely unaffected by the bank's analysis and billing system will remain unaffected by a change in customer float. Increasing float allocations to these customers simply reduces the perceived profitability of these accounts.

Each bank has a different mix of business customers who maintain excess balances and business customers who conscientiously manage their accounts. Generally, the more retail oriented a bank, the more likely it is to have business accounts whose deposit and withdrawal patterns are completely unaffected by the bank's account analysis system.

The allocation of float to interest bearing accounts has a direct impact on the interest expense of the bank. By paying interest on collected funds, rather than ledger balances, a bank can realize immediate benefit from float allocation, even if customers' deposit and withdrawal patterns are not affected. Most interest bearing accounts already enjoy a relatively long length of stay. Of course, this also means the level of uncollected funds in interest bearing accounts is generally lower than for business demand deposit accounts, and so proportionately less float can be allocated to reduce interest expense. Banks must also be careful not to allocate more float to interest bearing accounts than the bank actually incurs, in order to comply with Federal Reserve Regulation CC.

Allocation of float to noninterest bearing consumer accounts is usually less effective than allocation to business accounts or interest bearing accounts. The length of stay for most consumer deposits is already much longer than for business accounts, and consumer account pricing is usually based on minimum daily or average ledger balances instead of collected balances.

Coupling Float Reduction
with Float Allocation

We have reviewed float reduction efforts and float allocation efforts in the two previous sections. In each we assumed
a change in one area with no resulting change in the other. In
this section, we will review the benefits associated with float
reductions coupled with changes in float allocations.

Frequently, a bank will clear checks faster and pass on the
improved availability to customers. Determining the benefits
associated with such moves can be complex. Clearly, any float
reduction effort will tend to increase earnings, but what about
the accompanying change to customer availability?

One benefit associated with any improvement in customer availability is the marketing benefit of offering the
customer improved check collection. Of course, this benefit is
only important to those customers that understand and manage their collected balances. These customers will understand
and appreciate an improvement in funds availability. These
customers will also be most likely to withdraw funds sooner,
reducing their average length of stay and reducing any float
reduction related benefits to the bank.

Depending on the competitive nature of the bank's market
place, customer availability improvements can be an important consideration when soliciting new business and retaining existing business. Improvements in customer availability
that enhance a bank's ability to attract and retain profitable
customer relationships can be an effective marketing tool.

Not all customers understand and manage their collected
balances. Faster collection of checks deposited by these customers will result in a float reduction benefit even when
coupled with an improvement in customer availability. The
customer accounts that are generally unaffected by a change
in float allocation include interest bearing accounts that earn
interest on ledger balances rather than collected balances,
individual and nonanalyzed business accounts on which the
customer's service charges and fees are calculated without
considering collected balances, and all analyzed business
accounts that habitually maintain excess balance. Float reduction benefits are also realized on checks received from
nondepository sources such as loan payments or teller-cashed

checks.

To a large degree, the net benefit of float reductions passed on to customer is a function of which customer segments deposit the checks that are collected faster. In most large banks, a high percentage of transit items are deposited by cash management conscious customers, as opposed to consumers or business that keep excess balances. As a result, most of the benefits associated with coupling float reduction and float allocation efforts are passed through to cash management conscious customers in the form of improved availability. Obviously, such is not the case for a bank with a higher proportion of retail accounts.

Float Accounting and Balance Sheet Management

While float reduction and float allocation are the primary functions of float management, other float management techniques are being addressed by today's float managers. One of the most important of these nontraditional float management functions is float accounting and balance sheet management. By analyzing the way float is booked and categorized, a float manager can obtain substantial benefits for the bank.

Float Classification

Improper float classification can cost your bank money. Proper classification of float is important because float is a factor in determining a bank's reserve requirement and capital ratio. Improper float classification occurs when funds that could be classified as float are booked in a non-float category. Float related suspense accounts are most frequently misclassified as other assets.

Float's Role in Determining Reserve Requirements

Float plays an important role in determining reserve requirements. Commercial banks are required to maintain reserves in the form of vault cash and balances in the Federal Reserve Bank. **Reserve requirements** are currently set at 12 percent of net demand deposits and 3 percent of most time deposits. Net demand deposits are computed by subtracting

Cash Items in the Process of Collection (CIPC), the primary float account, from gross demand deposits.

Misclassification of float occurs when assets that meet the Federal Reserve definition of CIPC are classified in a category that is not deducted from gross demand deposits in the reserve calculation. Most frequently, this occurs with suspense accounts classified as "Other Assets." Float managers should review all debit balance suspense accounts with an eye toward classifying the suspense account as a float asset rather than as a non-float asset. Any resulting increase in the classification of float will reduce the level of reserves a bank must maintain by reducing the level of reservable deposits. A reduction in reserves, achieved by reclassifying an account from non-float to float, will allow a bank to increase earning assets and, thus, increase the bank's profitability.

Float's Role in Determining Capital Requirements

Float plays an important role in determining capital requirements. Under recently adopted risk-based capital guidelines, banks will be required to maintain capital equal to at least 8 percent of risk-adjusted assets. Assets are risk weighted by balance sheet classification. For example, commercial loans are weighted at 100 percent, so a bank must maintain capital equal to 8 percent of commercial loans. Federal Reserve Bank accounts and cash are weighted at 0 percent, so a bank is not required to hold risk based capital against these assets. Other risk weights vary, from 100 percent for most consumer loans, to 50 percent for mortgage loans, and 20 percent for certain highly liquid securities. Float is given a low 20 percent weighting, making the corresponding capital requirement 1.6 percent (20 percent x 8 percent = 1.6 percent).

Float managers should review all debit balance suspense accounts with an eye toward classifying the suspense account as a float asset rather than as a non-float asset. Any resulting decrease in assets that must be capitalized at up to 8 percent, accompanied by an offsetting increase in float, which must be capitalized at 1.6 percent, will reduce a bank's required capital. It is important to note that a reduction in capital requirements achieved by reclassifying an amount from non-float to float may not increase earnings, but it will increase the perceived stability of a bank as measured by its ability to maintain required capital. It also yields important benefits for balance sheet management, which will be discussed.

Balance Sheet Management

One of the most innovative areas of float management in recent years has been the development of balance sheet management techniques. **Balance sheet management** is the practice of reducing the amount of float on the bank's general ledger, thereby reducing total assets and boosting capital ratios. Balance sheet management accomplishes float reduction by coordinating the processing of deposits and payments with more advantageous posting of accounting entries.

Balance sheet float management differs from other float management efforts because the goal is to decrease capital requirements and to improve **Return on Assets (ROA)** and **Return on Equity (ROE)**, instead of actually increasing earnings by increasing investable funds. Prior to the implementation of risk-based capital guidelines, the impact of float levels on capital requirements was difficult to determine because regulators frequently established different capital requirements for different banks. Under risk-based capital requirements, float managers now face explicit equity cost allocations—opportunity costs of capital—against products and services that generate float. Previously, the float manager's main concerns were operating cost containment and obtaining compensation from customers who withdrew funds prior to collection.

The float manager can approximate the cost of capital associated with float balances under risk-based guidelines by using the following formula:

Float Balance x 20 percent Risk Weight x 8 percent Capital Requirement x 15 percent approximate ROE Goal = Annual Float Equity Capital Cost

The opportunity cost associated with using capital—a scarce resource in many banks—for float versus using capital for interest earning asset categories can be significant. If the float manager structures a product or service that adds $1,000,000 in float to the bank's books, the resulting increase in earnings required to yield a 15 percent ROE on the additional capital required to support the $1,000,000 in float would be $2,400 a year. In other words, the product or service that creates $1,000,000 in float must create $200 a month in after tax profits just to cover the capital cost of float. Of course, the explicit interest cost of float must also be taken into account, and the product or service would also require additional earnings to cover other costs.

Earlier Ledger Deadlines

The most effective way to reduce float on the balance sheet is to match more closely the timing of ledger credit and collected credit for deposited items. Typically, banks collect approximately 80 percent of a deposit in one day. The remaining 20 percent of items are split between on-us items that are available on the day of deposit and transit items that require two or three days to collect. As a result, the vast majority of a customer's deposit is available for withdrawal on the first business day after the deposit was made. Most banks post a deposit on the date received and carry float on the bank's books for about one day before passing collected credit to the depositing customer.

The **ledger deadline** is the latest time at which a bank will accept deposits or cash letters for same-day credit toward ledger balance. Most banks have late afternoon ledger deadlines for corporate deposits and incoming check deposits from other financial institutions. By moving the bank's ledger deadline to an earlier hour, before the bulk of the day's corporate and financial institution work is received, the bank can post customer deposits on the first business day after the deposit was made.

An earlier ledger deadline reduces bank float because it defers the booking of deposits, not because it defers customer availability of funds. When a bank moves its ledger deadline, it must usually change its published availability schedule accordingly. For example, items that are assigned one-day, if received before a 6:00 P.M. ledger deadline, would become same-day items if received after a new 2:00 P.M. deadline, but would be posted one day later. The customer would continue to enjoy the same availability of funds, but the bank would no longer have to carry the float on its balance sheet.

An earlier ledger deadline, perhaps 2:00 P.M., could eliminate a significant amount of a bank's float and provide a better matching of ledger balance and collected balance. Some banks may choose to only impose an early ledger deadline for corporate or correspondent bank customers who deliver deposits directly to the bank's processing centers, allowing individuals to make same day deposits until 4:00 P.M. or 6:00 P.M. in the branch.

Earlier direct deposit deadlines would not impact business customers who deposit in the branch rather than delivering checks directly to an operations center. One approach that allows for an earlier deadline for selected high volume branch customers is to accept these deposits at the branch in sealed packages that are forwarded unopened to the operations center. In this situation, the branch essentially acts as a package forwarder, with the customers' deposits being opened, receipted, and processed in the operations center rather than in the branch. As a result, a package accepted in the branch before 2:00 P.M. can be receipted in the operations center at 4:00 P.M. and processed for the following business day, thus reducing float association with the account.

As explained earlier, under an earlier ledger deadline, the customer incurs a change in float assignment on most items even though the customer incurs no change in availability for most deposited items. One-day items become same-day items, and two-day items become one-day items. Deposits are posted one day later, so availability is the same. But checks that were given same-day credit prior to the implementation of an earlier ledger deadline will be posted one day later with same day availability. In this case, the customer incurs a loss of availability. Some customers can outsort and deposit same day items separately for same day posting, allowing only the transit portion of the deposit to be deferred.

A second drawback of earlier ledger deadlines involves balance reporting. Because most deposits contain an average of about one day of float, many customers rely on previous day balance reporting to determine their investable cash position. Under an earlier ledger deadline environment, deposits are posted on the same day the bulk of funds become collected. As a result, the customer must receive same-day or intra-day balance reporting, as reliance on previous day balance reporting will be insufficient.

An earlier ledger deadline can yield significant float reductions if applied against a broad range of customers. But because of previously discussed drawbacks, some banks choose to be selective in their use of earlier ledger deadlines. Almost every bank has a few customer segments for which an earlier ledger deadline presents little or no drawbacks. Cash management customers using Depository Transfer Checks (DTCs) for cash concentration are a good example of a customer segment that can easily be placed on an earlier ledger deadline. DTCs are checks deposited in the concentration account to draw funds from outlying banks and therefore are always transit items, so they avoid the problems associated with same-day checks. And because DTC issuance is part of the cash management function, problems with balance reporting are minimized.

Late Evening Clearing House Exchange

A large part of a bank's float resides in an account entitled Clearing House Float or Clearing House Exchange. **Clearing house float** represents checks drawn on clearing house banks in the process of collection. Clearing house items taken for deposit on one day are normally exchanged and settled (paid for) on the following day, usually before 2:00 P.M. A late evening clearing house exchange is an attempt to exchange and settle clearing house items on the date of deposit rather than on the day following deposit.

Under this program, participating clearing house banks exchange checks after processing deposited checks but before posting entries to deposit accounts, usually around 10:00 P.M. or 11:00 P.M. Items received from the clearing house will be captured prior to posting and will be included as part of the current day's work.

Items received by a bank from other clearing house banks are considered payment for the items that it presents to member banks. The resulting entries are posted as a decrease in deposit liabilities and a decrease in clearing house float. These entries reflect the fact that other clearing house banks have paid for part, if not all, of the clearing house items presented against their banks. Because payment is made one day sooner, float is removed from the balance sheet.

One significant advantage of late evening clearing house exchange is the dual effect of balance sheet reduction and increased investable funds. Under late evening clearing house exchange, customer account balances are lowered to reflect earlier receipt of checks from other clearing house banks. Some customers, primarily those businesses with analyzed accounts, will replenish these funds to maintain a desired level of collected balances. As a result, late evening clearing house exchange will result in additional investable funds to participating banks.

Float Reporting

Float reporting is an important element of any serious float management effort. Without float reliable reporting, it is impossible to judge the results of float reduction and allocation efforts. Credible float reporting is also needed to ensure the ongoing commitment of the bank's senior management to the float program. Also, float reporting instills the type of discipline necessary to keep float management efforts vigorous and focused over the long term.

Although float is usually accounted for in standard financial reports, the information is buried. Float reporting focuses on the type of information needed to understand float within the bank and to support informed decision making about how to manage it. Float reporting also provides a way to monitor the progress of float management activities and to make adjustments as appropriate.

Float reporting is usually done on a monthly basis, with previous period statistics included for comparison and analysis of trends. A typical float report includes such data as aggregate float levels, aggregate demand deposit balances, and net usable funds to describe the overall float management environment. But the absolute amount of float depends to a great extent on factors outside the control of the float manager. For example, successful marketing of depository products will almost always result in an increase in float. As mentioned earlier, float is a by-product of a healthy bank. Most failing banks have a conspicuous absence of float, due to the difficulty of attracting deposits into a sinking institution.

The most important statistics in a float report are the ratios that are the principal indicators of the effectiveness of float management. The Clearing Ratio, for example, is an indicator of the average collection time for transit checks. All things being equal, a decrease in the clearing ratio means that the bank is collecting checks faster, and it is therefore reducing float. Float allocation is usually reported as a percentage of total float. Many banks allocate in excess of 100 percent of float, which creates negative float. Length of Stay, as mentioned earlier, can be an indicator of the effectiveness of float allocation.

However, float reporting ratios can be misleading; factors outside the control of float management can skew the statistics. Clearing ratios are affected by changes in the mix of checks deposited—receipt of more two and three-day checks will lengthen overall clearing times, even if collection of specific types of checks is improved. Shifts in deposit volumes between different customer categories can affect allocation percentages. Length of stay depends greatly on customer transaction patterns, and float allocation is only one of the factors influencing customer behavior.

Another factor that can skew float reporting is the fact that not all months are created equal. Months range in length from 28 to 31 days, creating an inherent inconsistency in monthly reporting periods. It takes more calendar days to collect checks over weekends and holidays, and the number of weekend days and holidays varies from month to month.

Float reporting should account for these and other variables so that the monthly float report can be seen as a credible, valuable management information tool. Chapter 8 describes an approach to float reporting that gives float managers a way to account for changes in volume, clearing times, and deposit mix.

Float reporting is like any other type of management reporting. It should be concise, functional, and straightforward. The best way to present float statistics is often in the form of charts and graphs. The float report should present information that is essential to understanding float and to making decisions about float management. Nonessential information should be left out.

This final point is important. In the context of float reporting, nonessential information is anything that is not essential to the reader of the report, not the writer. A float manager must have access to great volumes of data about check clearings, float account balances and so forth, but the float report is not intended for the float manager. The float report is usually intended for senior management of such areas as operations, cash management, and financial management, as well as for selected middle managers of functional areas with an interest in float. Don't bury important float information under a mountain of numbers.

Float Accounting 3

Bank Float is a sum of money, recorded on the financial books of a bank, representing checks and other financial instruments that are outstanding and in the process of collection. As explained in this definition, float becomes **bank float** when it is recorded on the books of a bank. Until the bank receives and records a deposit, it is not a participant in the float cycle. Float accounting is, therefore, an essential element of float management. Float accounting is the way a bank identifies and keeps track of float.

Float accounting provides the information needed to make decisions about all aspects of float management, including float reduction and float allocation. It is the basis for good float reporting, and it is the primary tool used in float allocation and balance sheet management. And as explained in chapter 2, good float accounting can produce substantial benefits by ensuring that float is categorized correctly for the computation of required reserves and minimum capital ratios. Therefore, a thorough knowledge of float accounting is vital for anyone involved in float management. This chapter explains the fundamental concepts and accounts used in float accounting.

Accounting policies and accounting treatment of float will vary from bank to bank. The accounting treatment used in this chapter may vary from the accounting treatment used by your bank. The purpose of the treatment used in this chapter is to explain the fundamental nature of the recorded transaction and to show a simple set of entries that illustrate how float accounting is applied. The objective is to provide a conceptual framework against which your bank's accounting can be understood.

Float accounting varies in the level of detail used to record bank float and to track work in process. A single set of entries may be made representing the entire day's processing, or separate entries may be made for each source of work received or for each processing area or unit. Some banks generate entries for various time periods or for each operating shift. The names of float accounts also vary significantly among banks.

The Paying Bank's Perspective

The payment of a check is the final step in the float cycle. Paying banks are obligated to pay for checks drawn against themselves, known as **on-us items**. The paying bank, in turn, seeks payment from its customer. The role of the float manager, from the paying bank perspective, is to ensure that the customer pays for a check on the same day that the bank pays for the item.

Accounting for items in the process of collection—float— from the paying bank perspective covers two basic activities. First, a paying bank must pay for the on-us checks it receives, a process known as settlement, and then the paying bank must post the items against the appropriate customers' accounts. We will review the accounting treatment for the three major sources of paid items:

- On-us Deposits.
- Inclearings.
- Clearing House.

On-Us Deposits

If you were to write a check on your account and deposit this check back into your account, your account balance would remain unchanged, even though a deposit was credited and a check was paid against your account. From a bank's perspective, a similar phenomenon occurs when one customer deposits a different customer's check. The total money in the bank remains unchanged, even though one account increases and one account decreases. These transactions are generally called **on-us deposits**.

The accounting entries for a $1,000 on-us deposit are as follows:

Debit: Transaction Account—Customer A $1,000

Credit: Transaction Account—Customer B $1,000

Transaction accounts are carried as liabilities under one of the "Deposit" categories on the bank's balance sheet. A credit increases the transaction account to which the deposit is posted and a debit decreases the transaction account to which the paid item is posted. The bank's investable funds remain unchanged, as the bank does not pay any outside party for on-us items deposited. It is important to understand that a bank's usable funds can only be reduced by moving money out of the bank, usually out of its Federal Reserve account or an account at a correspondent bank. In the on-us deposit, no such transfer occurs.

Inclearings

When a check is presented to the Federal Reserve Bank for clearing, the Federal Reserve collects the check by withdrawing money from the paying bank's Federal Reserve account and by presenting the items to that bank. The on-us items a bank receives from the Federal Reserve are referred to as **inclearings**. All banks receive inclearings either directly from the Federal Reserve or through a correspondent bank.

The accounting entries for $1,000 in inclearings are as follows:

Debit: Various Transaction Accounts $1,000

Credit: Due-from Fed: Reserve Account $1,000

A Due-from Fed: Reserve Account is an asset account in the Cash and Due-from category, which represents the bank's cash account at the Federal Reserve Bank. A credit to the Federal Reserve account is a reduction in the account balance. The credit reflects the reduction that has occurred in the bank's reserve account when the Federal Reserve Bank withdrew money as payment for inclearings presented. Debits to the various transactions accounts are reductions in the customers' account balances to pay for the checks that they have written.

In most banks, the entries associated with inclearings may flow through an inclearings account for control purposes as follows:

1. Debit: Inclearings $1,000

   Credit: Due-From Fed: Reserve Account $1,000

2. Debit: Various Transaction Accounts $1,000

   Credit: Inclearings $1,000

The Inclearings account is an asset account, usually in the "Cash and Due-from" category. Accounting for inclearings with two sets of entries allows the first entry to be generated when the inclearings are received and captured and the second entry to be generated when the various transaction accounts are posted. These entries frequently occur on separate operating shifts, even though they occur on the same business day. The inclearings account should end each day with a zero balance. A balance in an inclearings account would imply that checks were received and paid for, but not yet posted to customer accounts.

Banks also receive on-us items from commercial banks, many of which are clearing banks for other institutions. If the paying bank has a correspondent account with the presenting bank, the accounting and settlement could be accomplished in much the same manner as with Federal Reserve inclearings. Instead of crediting Due-from Fed, the paying bank credits Due-from Correspondent Banks.

Such arrangements, however, are rare. More common is the case where the presenting bank has an account with the paying bank. Such an account, known as a Due-to Correspondent Bank account, serves as a depository account for the items. A **Due-to account** is essentially the same as any other customer transaction account, and so the transaction is treated as an on-us deposit. The accounting is similar to the on-us deposit example, with the transaction account classified under the category "Due-to Banks."

Clearing House Exchange

Banks often exchange checks among themselves without the use of due-to/due-from correspondent bank accounts. Such an arrangement is normally referred to as a **clearing house exchange** or city clearings. Most clearing house arrangements operate within a local area or region. Clearing house exchange minimizes the impact to a bank's reserve account associated with receiving and paying for on-us items deposited with other local banks. This is achieved by a process called **net settlement**. Under net settlement, banks exchange checks or other items and make or receive a single payment for the difference in value between the items they present and the items they receive, instead of making or receiving payment for the full value of each presentment separately.

In an example of net settlement, Bank A has $90 of items drawn on Bank B, and Bank B has $110 of items drawn on Bank A. If both banks presented these items to the Federal Reserve for clearing, each would pay for its inclearings by having its reserve account lowered by the gross amount of the items involved—$110 for Bank A and $90 for Bank B. Under net settlement through a clearing house exchange, Bank A and Bank B would exchange items directly; and after calculating net settlement, Bank A would pay Bank B the $20 difference. The $20 payment is made by transferring money or reserves from Bank A's Federal Reserve account into Bank B's Federal Reserve account. In effect, Bank A has paid Bank B for its $110 in checks with $20 in money and $90 in items drawn on Bank B. Likewise, B has paid for its $90 in items with $110 in checks and received $20 in money from Bank B to make up the deficit.

Bank A's accounting entries for the clearing exchange are as follows:

1. Debit: Clearing House Exchange ... $ 90

   Credit: Various Transaction Accounts ... $ 90

2. Debit: Various Transaction Accounts ... $110

   Credit: Clearing House Exchange ... $110

3. Debit: Clearing House Exchange $20

   Credit: Due From Fed: Reserve Account $20

The entries reflect the clearing house exchange entries from Bank A's perspective. Entry one shows how Bank A obtained the items—the checks were taken for deposit—and how the items were cleared through the clearing house. Entry 2 reflects the receipt of on-us items from the clearing house and the posting of those items to transaction accounts. Entry 3 reflects the net settlement transaction in which Bank A's Federal Reserve account was reduced by $20 as payment for the difference between $110 in on-us items received and the $90 in checks presented. After all three sets of entries, the clearing house account will have a zero balance. Most clearing house exchanges involve more than two banks, making calculation of net settlement more complex. But the accounting is essentially the same as in the example for the individual banks.

The clearing house float account will nearly always carry a positive balance because the first set of entries normally occurs on one business day while the second and third set of entries normally occur on the following business day. This occurs because most checks received for deposit one day are cleared in the following day's exchange. Late night clearing house exchange is an exception where at least some items deposited at clearing house banks are exchanged the same day, although final settlement, represented by the third set of entries, still occurs later.

Paying Bank Float

Payment procedures are not designed to create float. If everything works perfectly, there is no float created in the payment process. But everything almost never works perfectly. Float is created in the payment process when the bank is unable to post an item to a customer account on the same day that the bank pays for the item. When paying bank float occurs, the float manager should seek ways to pass the float cost on to the customers responsible.

The accounting for paying bank float usually involves the use of a suspense account. Regardless of how on-us checks enter the bank—on-us deposits, inclearings, or clearing house exchange—the items are destined to be posted against customer accounts. If for any reason the items cannot be posted, they will be debited to a suspense account, usually called "Unposted Items." The items are posted to customers' accounts the following day or returned unpaid. Some common reasons for unposted items are closed accounts, invalid account number, stop payment orders, and insufficient funds.

The Clearing Bank's Perspective

Banks create **check clearing float** when checks are taken for deposit and credited to customers' accounts prior to receipt of available funds for the items. Accounting for float—items in the process of collection—from the clearing bank's perspective involves the tracking of funds through the collection process. We will review the accounting treatment for three common means of collecting checks; namely, Federal Reserve Bank clearing, Correspondent Bank clearing, and, Clearing House Exchange.

Federal Reserve Bank Clearing

The Federal Reserve System handles between 30 and 40 percent of all transit check collections. Most banks large enough to employ a float manager will clear some checks through the Federal Reserve. Federal Reserve Banks handle customer float assignments through the use of a deferred account and a reserve account. This process is significantly different from the way commercial banks handle customer float allocation.

At the Federal Reserve Bank, a depositing bank's reserve account represents collected funds only. Only entries with same-day availability are posted to this account. Any next-day or subsequent-day entries are posted to the deferred account. Balances roll from the deferred account into the reserve account on the effective date or date of collection. As a result, the accounting entries for most checks cleared through the Federal Reserve Bank will flow through the deferred account before being posted to the reserve account.

A bank's account is posted from a "rainbow sheet" rather than from a deposit ticket. Each depositing bank provides its

Federal Reserve branch with a rainbow sheet summarizing all of the day's check clearing activity with each Federal Reserve branch, with separate totals for each availability category. The local Federal Reserve will use the rainbow sheet to post entries to the deferred account and later transfer balances from the deferred account into the reserve account.

The accounting entries for $1,000 in Federal Reserve clearings are as follows:

1. Debit: Due-from Fed: Deferred Account $1,000

   Credit: Various Transaction Accounts $1,000

2. Debit: Due-from Fed: Reserve Account $1,000

   Credit: Due-from Fed: Deferred Account $1,000

The first entry shows how the bank obtained the items—checks taken for deposit—and how the items were cleared through the Federal Reserve System. The first entry remains unchanged even when the bank clears items directly with other Federal Reserve branches. The second entry reflects the fact that deferred balances have become collected and that the funds have moved from the deferred account into the reserve account. The second entry will occur on a day following the date of the first entry. Same-day items, such as U.S. Treasury checks deposited before 2:00 P.M., post directly to the reserve account without flowing through the deferred account.

The reserve account is at the heart of a bank's funds management efforts. In most banks, the area responsible for managing the cash balances in the reserve account is called the "money desk" or the "Federal Reserve desk." The primary job of the money desk is to maintain enough cash in the reserve account to meet reserve requirements and intra-day funding needs, while investing any excess cash balances.

Correspondent Bank Clearings

Many large banks clear checks for other large banks and for downstream, or smaller banks. Most banks clear checks through at least one correspondent bank. Some large check clearing banks may clear checks through scores of other banks. Accounting for checks collected through a correspondent differs from Federal Reserve clearing in one important way. Unlike the Federal Reserve, correspondent banks generally give ledger credit on the date of deposit, but allocate float to reduce available funds. With the Federal Reserve method of deferred accounting, funds availability is based on how the rainbow sheet is filled out, whereas with correspondent bank deposit accounting, funds availability is based on the customer's float assignment at the time of deposit. In both cases, availability and pricing is consistent with published or agreed to schedules, and funds availability is usually subject to adjustments.

The accounting entries for $1,000 in correspondent bank clearings are as follows:

1. Debit: Due-from Correspondent $1,000

   Credit: Various Transaction Accounts $1,000

2. Debit: Due-from Fed: Reserve Account
   $1,000

   Credit: Due-from Correspondent $1,000

   The first entry shows how the bank obtained the checks through customer deposits and how the items were cleared through a correspondent bank. The second entry shows collected funds being moved from the correspondent bank into the reserve account. Normally, this transfer occurs through a wire transfer. Once the funds are in the reserve account, the funds can be invested. The date of the second entry is dependent on when the deposited funds become available and may be spread over two or three different business days. If checks are cleared through a correspondent, the depositing bank will normally withdraw or wire out each day's available balance. Each day's available balance will consist of today's same-day funds, yesterday's one-day funds, and day before yesterday's two-day funds, all net of any adjusting entries.
   Note: The accounting for clearing house exchange from the paying bank perspective was covered in the paying bank perspective section. The accounting entries from the clearing

bank perspective are the same.

Should Float Be Considered an Asset?

Generally accepted accounting practices classify float as an asset. Float is viewed as an asset because float represents checks—claims to money that will be collected and converted into money in a manner similar to accounts receivable. Classifying float as an asset inflates a bank's balance sheet, an effect that at one time was viewed as positive and a sign of a healthy bank. But with the greater attention paid to Return on Assets and capital ratios, inflation of assets has become undesireable.

More recently, some critics have argued that float should not be treated as an asset. The premise for this argument is based on a reconsideration of when it is appropriate to record the creation of a deposit liability between bank and customer. Most individuals believe that a deposit liability exists on the date of deposit. With this understanding, float must be classified as an asset. Most businesses, however, understand the difference between the ledger balance and the collected balance in their accounts. With this understanding, the collected balance, not the ledger balance, represents the true liability between bank and customer. This is the justification for penalizing customers for drawing checks against uncollected funds.

Assuming the collected balance, rather than the ledger balance, represents the true liability between bank and customer, classifying float as an asset is inanappropriate, because doing so mis-states the bank's true liabilities. Under the alternative approach, float would be classified as a contra-liability. A contra-liability reduces the balances in liability accounts, instead of creating an offsetting asset. Such treatment would reduce the bank's balance sheet, an effect that generally would be viewed as favorable in today's banking environment.

The ability to classify float as a contra-liability must be addressed from a financial reporting perspective, as well as from a regulatory perspective. Because banks have historically recorded a liability on the date of deposit, rather than upon collection of deposited items, recognition of the collected balance as the true liability between bank and customer would require a clear understanding between the bank and its customers. Once agreements were obtained, float could be classified as a contra-liability for financial reporting purposes. Obtaining approval to classify float as a contra-liability from a regulatory perspective is not so simple. In the past, the regulators have denied requests to view float as anything other than an asset. To date, no bank has chosen to report different levels of assets and liabilities for financial reporting versus regulatory reporting. As a result, float remains classified as an asset on banks' books.

Float Allocation 4

Float is a necessary by-product of banking. If a bank is in the business of accepting deposits or loan payments, it will incur float. No amount of float reduction efforts will get rid of all the float on a bank's books.

Although float is inevitable, it is also costly. Float allocation gives banks a way to recoup the cost of float by passing it on to the depositors, products, and internal departments that create it. Float allocation is one of the most powerful tools of float management; effective float allocation is often what distinguishes the superior float management program from the mediocre.

Float allocation yields three main benefits:

1. Float allocation can influence the behavior of customers and bank managers. Funds availability restrictions increase customer account length of stay, while internal float allocation discourages practices that create float.

2. Float allocation can increase revenues or decrease interest expense directly, if fees, service charges, and interest are based on collected balances instead of ledger balances.

3. Float allocation allows more accurate analysis of the profitability of customer accounts, business units, and products.

Float allocation can be viewed as a "top down" process that follows two paths. Along one path, float is allocated to managerial units and customers within the managerial units. Along the other, float is allocated to product lines. Table 4.1 illustrates this concept. This chapter looks at three aspects of float allocation within this framework: customer float allocation, product float allocation, and allocation to managerial or business units.

Figure 4.1   Float Allocation

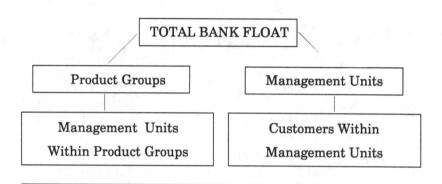

Customer Float Allocation

Allocation of float at the customer level is critical to the determination of customer profitability. Allocation is particularly important when significant differences exist between customers regarding their deposit and withdrawal habits, and when significant differences exist between the type and mix of items deposited. This is the case with most business accounts. Consumer accounts are a much more homogeneous group. As a result, most banks make little effort to allocate deposit float to consumer deposits at the individual account level, except in the case of interest bearing accounts.

When banks first began associating float with depositors, the float allocated to a customer was normally equal to or less than the actual time required to collect deposited checks. The practice of assigning a customer float of two days when the item could be collected in one day was considered inappropriate. System limitations also contributed to a tendency to under-allocate float. For example, if a portion of checks drawn on banks in a particular city could be collected in one day, with the rest requiring two days, the bank would assign one-day float to all such items because it had no way of determining which items would take longer.

Today, most banks view customer float allocation as a form of pricing. Assigning a customer two days of float when the item is collected in one day allows the bank to offer a lower per item price or increase the profitability of the account. Negative float, the allocation of more float to accounts than the bank incurs, is an essential element of bank pricing, especially for business accounts. There is, however, one significant restriction on the allocation of negative float to interest bearing accounts. Under the Expedited Funds Availability Act (Federal Reserve Regulation CC), interest on transaction accounts must reflect availability at least as good as that received by the bank. This rule does not, however, apply to account analysis.

Float Allocation Methods

There are three common methods for allocating float to accounts: float factors, float tables, and float tickets.

The simplest method of float assignment, and consequently one of the first used by banks, is through the use of float factors. Using this float factor method, a bank multiplies deposits by a factor that approximates the average number of days required to clear deposited items. A single float factor can be used for all bank deposits or different float factors can be used for different customers or account segments. The factor can be based on overall bank collection times, or it can be based on samples of deposits from each account segment or individual customer.

For example, if a bank determines that the average deposit incurs 1.2 days float, the bank would use a float factor of 1.2. For a $10,000 deposit, the bank would allocate $12,000 of float to the customer. On a float-day basis, this would equal $10,000 of one-day float and $2,000 of two-day float, so the customer's collected funds would be calculated as follows:

	Ledger Balance	Allocated Float	Collected Balance
Date of Deposit	$10,000	$10,000	0
Day One	$10,000	$2,000	$8,000
Day Two	$10,000	0	$10,000

The main advantage of float factor allocation is its simplicity. There is no need to determine the composition of each deposit, because all deposits, including cash, incur the same float. The information needed to assign float—total deposits posted to each account—is readily available from even the most basic deposit account systems.

But the float factor method of allocation has some serious drawbacks. It is an inherently imprecise method of allocating float to specific deposits and customers. Customers that deposit mostly cash and local checks will be allocated substantially more float than they generate, while those that deposit more out-of-state checks will incur less than their share. For this reason, float factor allocation is subject to numerous case-by-case exceptions that reduce its effectiveness as a tool for daily balance management. It is difficult, for example, to explain to customers why cash deposits are subject to more than one day of float.

Float factors also have a tendency to lag changes in deposit mix, making them inaccurate even at the bank level over time. If customers increase the proportion of items that they deposit with two-day collection times, the float factor will understate actual float. Float factor allocation is even subject to manipulation by sophisticated customers. A customer with accounts at several banks may deposit a disproportionate share of its two-day checks in a bank that uses an attractive float factor.

Because of the deficiencies in the float factor method of allocation, its use has been declining rapidly in recent years. Few financial institutions use float factors for daily account allocation and calculation of collected funds. However, float factors are still used by a significant number of smaller institutions for periodic float calculations, such as computation of monthly account analysis, where precision on a deposit-by-deposit basis is less critical. Float factors can also be useful in a bank's internal planning and analysis, where actual collection data can be used to develop float factors that are then used to estimate such things as product profitability and departmental allocation of float costs.

Float table allocation is a more precise and flexible method for allocating float to deposits. This method uses actual data captured by the check processing system to determine the float associated with each check in a deposit. Float is then allocated to each deposit according to the types of checks the deposit includes.

The same $10,000 deposit used in the previous example might have included the following items:

- One check for $1,000 drawn on the depositary bank, which incurs no float.
- Three checks for a total of $6,000 drawn on other local banks, which incur one-day float.
- One check for $3,000 drawn on a remote bank, which incurs two-day float.

The float allocation system would identify each deposited check, locate the appropriate float allocation in the float table, and calculate total 0-day, one-day, and two-day float for the deposit. Collected balances would be calculated as follows:

	Ledger Balance	Allocated Float	Collected Balance
Date of Deposit	$10,000	$9,000	$1,000
Day One	$10,000	$3,000	$7,000
Day Two	$10,000	0	$10,000

In this example, a total of $12,000 in float was allocated to the deposit:

$$\$6,000 \times 1 \text{ day} = \$6,000$$
$$\$3,000 \times 2 \text{ days} = \$6,000$$
$$\$12,000 \text{ Total Float}$$

$12,000 is the same amount of float allocated under the float factor method for this example, but the float table allocation was more precise, because the customer was given same-day collected balances for the $1,000 on-us check deposit. If the deposit mix had been different, with more or less two-day or same-day items, the two methods would have allocated different float to the deposit.

A bank may use a single float table for all deposits, or it may have different float tables for different customer segments. Sophisticated customers that are highly sensitive to availability may even negotiate float concessions that require account-specific float tables. The use of multiple float tables is a powerful tool for attracting high-volume depository customers.

Use of the float table method of allocation was once restricted by the limitations of banks' check processing or deposit systems. Today, however, most systems used by even small financial institutions are capable of float table allocation. More sophisticated systems include refinements such as the ability to maintain multiple float tables, assign different availability based on time-of-day or day-of-week, adjust float allocation to account for missed deadlines, and assign fractional float.

Float tickets are used to allocate float to accounts directly, or for float adjustments. Float ticket allocation is not an alternative to the float table or float factor methods, but it is a way of augmenting the basic float allocation system.

Although the bulk of float can be associated with customer deposits, there are other activities that incur float as well. Returned item handling, stop payment orders, and payable-through draft processing are just a few of the services that can generate float. Banks allocate float for these activities to customers by entering float tickets. Float tickets can also be used to correct float allocation errors and to adjust float allocations to account for factors such as missed check clearing deadlines.

Allocating Paying Bank Float to Customers

Float is created in the payment process when the bank is unable to post checks against customer accounts on the same day the bank pays for the items. When paying bank float occurs, the float manager should seek ways to pass the float cost to customers responsible.

Checks the bank cannot post against customers accounts are usually debited to a suspense account called "Unposted Items." Some common reasons for unposted items are closed accounts, invalid account numbers, stop payment orders, and insufficient funds. The float manager should review all unposted accounts with an eye towards allocating the cost of carrying unposted items to the appropriate customers.

Some paying bank float cannot or should not be passed back to customers. A check drawn on a closed account is an example of an item that creates float for the paying bank. While the paying bank can return the check, the paying bank must fund the item from the day it makes payment until it is returned. For the one day it holds the item, the paying bank holds a sterile, noninterest earning asset and incurs an associated opportunity cost. In the case of a check returned because the account has been closed, float cannot be allocated to the customer because no customer exists. In this example, the bank incurs paying bank float that must be viewed as part of the cost of doing business.

Some paying bank float can, however, be passed on to customers. The benefits associated with such float allocation can be significant. The amount of float associated with unposted debits can be quite large. Items with invalid account numbers, for example, must be researched and then posted to the correct account. The bank incurs at least one day of float in this transaction. This float can be passed on to the customer. In addition, allocating unposted item float to the customer can be accomplished by adjusting the customer's collected account balance. Some banks automate this adjustment process.

Most banks post such items using a special transaction code that force posts the debit. Force posting ensures that the item will not be rejected for such reasons as insufficient funds. The posting system can be designed to create a one day collected balance adjustment for each force post transaction. This process will allow the customer, rather than the bank, to bear the float costs associated with unposted items.

Fraud Prevention

A by-product of customer float allocation is that it can help detect and prevent certain types of check fraud, particularly check kiting. A check kite is a fraudulent scheme that takes advantage of check collection float to obtain the use of funds which appear to be on deposit but do not actually exist.

Check kiting schemes typically employ several checking

accounts at different banks. The check kiter begins the process by writing a check drawn against insufficient funds on the account at one bank, and depositing the check into the account at another bank. The kiter then writes a check on the second account, drawing against the uncollected funds from the first worthless check. The check on the second account is either deposited into the first account to cover the initial check, or used to fund a third account. Eventulally, the first check is covered, completing the circle. By repeating this process, often with many variations to disguise the pattern, a skilled check kiter can parlay an insignificant initial account balance into large sums of fictitious money. The funds are then withdrawn, leaving one or more banks with losses. Check kiting can also be used to create balances that are in effect an unauthorized, interest-free loan, which is later repaid by the deposit of actual funds. An example of this type activity was the elaborate check kite operated by broker E. F. Hutton in the early 1980s.

By allocating float to customer accounts, banks can sometimes identify accounts that systematically draw on uncollected funds. More advanced kite suspect detection systems look for the type of deposit and withdrawal patterns that are typical of kiting. Once detected, a bank can attempt to stop the kite by restricting withdrawal of check deposits. On an everyday basis, banks can help prevent kiting and minimize potential kiting losses by allowing the withdrawal of only collected funds.

Product Float Allocation

Product management and product profitability measurement were relatively late arrivals to banking, but they have already made a significant impact on the way banks do business. The purpose of product management is to optimize profitability by product line in much the same way that customer profitability analysis allows closer scrutiny and management of profitability by customer. Banks that have developed strong product management functions generally have been quite pleased with the financial results. Individual product components, however, are frequently more interdependent than are individual customers. As a result, while total bank profitability is usually maximized by maximizing individual customer profitability, total bank profitability may not be maximized by maximizing individual product profitability. This is the nature of "loss leaders" and products required to fill out a complete product line family.

Float is allocated to bank products for two primary reasons. First, it is important to understand the costs associated with carrying sterile assets and the cost of capital associated with float. Second, float allocation is generally considered to be an effective method to generate additional earnings through negative float revenue. Some products are better able to generate negative float than others. If float is allocated to products with an explicit cost, and negative float becomes a revenue stream, product managers are able to include the value of float in their analyses. The result is that product management decisions are better informed and more likely to enhance the overall profitability of the bank.

An example of how float allocation can influence product management is seen when the manager must decide whether to pass float reductions obtained through faster check collection on to check customers. Without float allocation, product managers don't have an incentive to keep float reduction benefits as negative float. Instead, they are likely to pass all savings on as availability schedule improvements—a product enhancement. But if negative float is credited to the products that generate it, product managers might pass on availability only when it truly improves the competitiveness of the product and retain negative float as an earnings enhancement in other cases.

Most float is allocated to depository products, because most float is created when banks accept deposits. Some products generate proportionately more float than others, including check clearing for other banks and lockbox services. Nondepository products can also generate considerable float, however, especially consumer lending products such as mortgages, credit cards, and automobile finance. Most consumers make monthly payments by check; and because these products are often sold to customers with no existing relationship with the bank, many of the checks received are transit items and therefore generate float.

Many of our current depository products and services

were developed in a era when the interest and capital costs of float were difficult to understand and measure. As a result, many products do not attempt to minimize float. In today's environment, the float manager must work with the product manager to structure products and services that minimize capital requirements and maximize ROA and ROE. One approach becoming more common is to structure high-volume check products to minimize balance sheet impact. This can be accomplished by such tactics as accepting same-day items for same day posting and separating and accepting next day items for next day posting. While such a structure may be a little more complicated for some customers, such an approach will minimize the balance sheet costs associated with attracting the high-volume check deposits.

Earlier ledger deadlines and changes to depository product offerings are product changes with significant float reduction potential. These float management techniques will become increasingly more common as bank management begins to understand better the explicit and implicit costs associated with float. Today, float managers work with product managers to reduce the float created by products without an accompanying reduction in earnings. Likewise, product managers are eager to reduce the float associated with their products when doing so improves product profitability. Product float allocation provides the mechanism for including the interest and capital costs of float in the calculation of product profitability. In this way, float management is integrated into the management of the products that create float. Chapter 9 takes this process one step further, by exploring the concept of managing float itself as a depository product.

Managerial Unit Float Allocation

Most banks calculate the profitability of branches, lending operations, and other managerial or business units. The manager responsible for each unit is usually given a profitability goal for each budget period. Compensation and advancement are often based to a large extent on performance in meeting profitability goals. In addition to profitability goals, managers are usually evaluated according to other quantitative measures, such as loan growth, sales, and cost control. Operating and profitability objectives are often included in incentive programs for managers and their units.

By allocating float to managerial units, a bank can include the cost of float in the calculation of unit profitability. Including float allocation in such performance measures serves two purposes. It ensures that the calculation more accurately reflect the unit's impact on overall bank earnings by including the cost of float. It also encourages managers to work toward reducing float, and it discourages practices that create float.

For the most part, managerial unit float allocation is accomplished simply by accumulating the aggregate deposit float levels associated with a managerial unit's customers base. However, not all float is deposit float. Some bank float is created from nondeposit sources. Banks sometimes ignore this float in their allocation, or allocate all nondeposit float to a single overhead unit. If the aggregate amount of a banks's nondeposit float is small, such a practice may be appropriate. But if nondeposit float levels are significant, the bank should try to allocate it to the responsible units.

A few examples of nondeposit float that can be allocated to managerial units are:

- Cashed out check float—allocated to the branch.

- Loan payment float—allocated to the lending unit.

- Safe Deposit Box payment float—allocated to the branch housing the safe deposit box.

- Treasury Tax and Loan (TT&L) float—allocated to branches that accept transit items for TT&L payments.

Optimizing
Check Collection 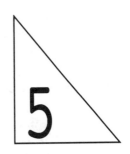 5

Checks in the process of collection are the largest source of bank float, and it is easy to see why. Americans write more than 50 billion checks a year, more than 10 times the volume of any other type of noncash payment. Float is inherent in the check collection process because checks must be transported to the bank on which they are drawn for collection.

A check can be drawn on any one of more than 20,000 financial institutions in the United States, and it can usually be collected through a variety of alternative clearing agents. With such volume and complexity in the check collection system, it makes sense that careful analysis and optimization of check clearing is central to float management.

In order to understand the concepts and techniques of check clearing optimization, it is necessary to understand the check collection system.

The Check Collection System

A **check** is a negotiable demand draft payable at a financial institution. This definition of a check includes three important provisions that govern check collection.

1. A check is negotiable; namely, it can be transferred from one party to another.

2. It is a demand draft; namely it is a claim to money that is converted to money when it is presented to the payor.

3. It is payable at a financial institution, so it must be delivered to a bank, thrift, or other financial institution for collection.

In other words, checks are collected by being delivered to financial institutions, and often they are delivered through intermediaries. Check collection intermediaries, also known as clearing agents, play an essential role in the check collection process, because no bank has the resources to deliver checks directly to every paying institution. Only the Federal Reserve System presents checks to all payor banks. Therefore, the selection of clearing agents is an important element of check collection optimization.

Checks can be drawn on commercial banks, savings banks, savings and loan associations, credit unions, Federal Reserve Banks, or Federal Home Loan Banks. In the interest of simplicity, the term "bank" will be used to refer to any financial institution on which checks are drawn. There are also a variety of drafts that, although payable at a bank, are not truly checks. These include drafts that are "payable through" or "payable at" a bank, but are actually drawn on the treasury of a corporation or governmental entity. Also, U.S. Treasury checks, travelers cheques, and money orders often are drawn on entities other than banks. Most such items, however, are collected as cash items in much the same way as checks. Therefore, the term "check" will be used to refer to any items that are collected as cash items.

The check collection system has been automated to a significant extent, with high-speed equipment reading and sorting checks. This has been made possible by **Magnetic Ink Character Recognition (MICR)**, a technology that allows automated equipment to read numbers and symbols imprinted on checks with a special ink. The MICR line—the area on a check reserved for MICR characters—runs along the bottom edge of the item's face, as shown in Figure 5.1. The bank on which a check is drawn is identified by a routing number in the MICR line. The **routing number** identifies each paying bank uniquely, as well as the bank's Federal Reserve district, branch, and check processing region.

The check collection process for banks begins when checks are received in customers' deposits. The depositary bank cannot capture or sort the checks until the dollar amount is imprinted on each item in the MICR line. This is done through the process of **proof encoding**. Operators using special machines encode the amount on each item in magnetic ink,

Figure 5.1

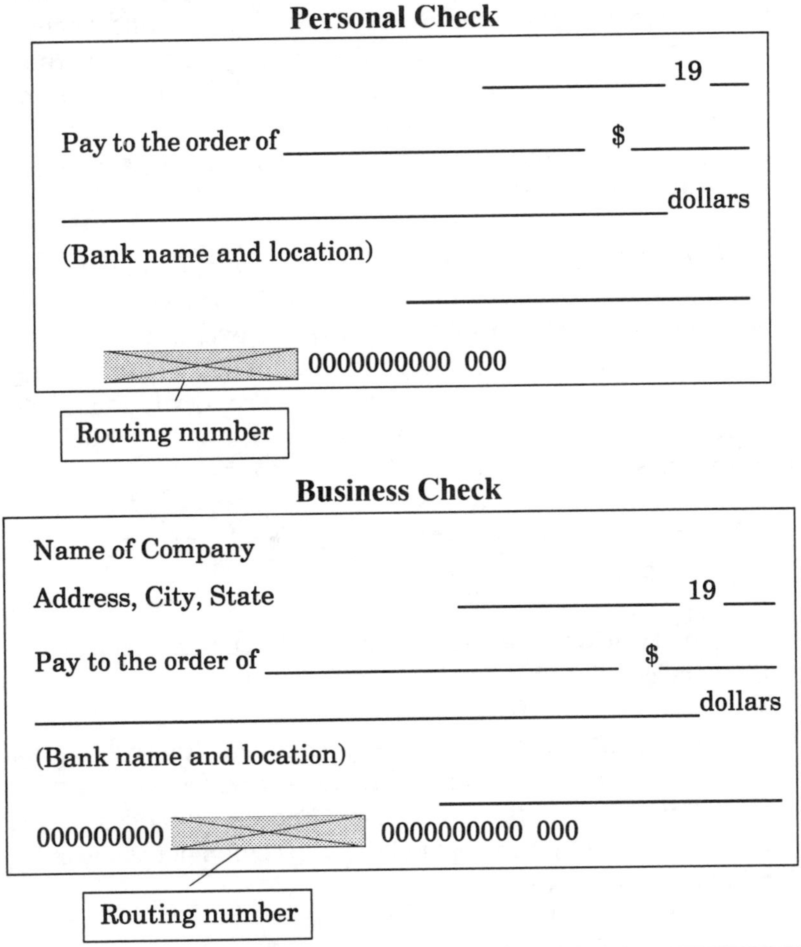

Personal Check

Business Check

while the machine totals debits and credits to show proof that deposits are in balance.

The bank then processes the checks on a reader/sorter, which reads the MICR line on each item, captures the data for posting and float assignment, sorts on-us checks and deposit tickets from transit items, and sorts transit items according to destination—all at speeds as fast as 35 miles an hour. Banks often collect checks through more clearing agents than they have pockets for on their reader/sorters, so the items have to be sorted again, a process known as "repassing." Through a series of passes and repasses, the checks are sorted into bundles for delivery to clearing agents and paying banks. Each bundle, accompanied by a listing of checks and deposit documents, is called a **cash letter**. Cash letters are than dispatched to their destinations, usually via courier or other means that assures rapid delivery.

Banks can choose from among several alternatives for check collection:

- **Clearing Houses**—associations of financial institutions that exchange checks on a regular basis. The clearing house association establishes rules for exchanging items, sets exchange deadlines, and provides for settlement among its members. Most clearing houses are local, including financial institutions within a single city or metropolitan area, or region, covering part or all of a state.

- **Direct Presentment**—delivery of checks directly to the paying bank for collection.

- **Correspondent Banks**—banks that provide check clearing services to other banks for a fee.

- **The Federal Reserve System**—Federal Reserve banks clear checks for financial institutions for a fee. Banks may clear checks through their own Federal Reserve Bank branch, or through the branch for the region of the bank on which the items are drawn.

Most banks optimize check clearing by using a combination of these methods to collect checks.

The most efficient and least costly way to collect checks drawn on local banks is usually through the clearing house. Banks generally exchange checks through a clearing house free of charge, though the clearing house association usually assesses dues or allocates its cost of operation among members. Clearing houses also offer the advantage of net settlement, which eliminates the need for due-from and due-to accounts for clearing. Checks received by the bank one day generally are exchanged through the clearing house for settlement the following day.

Banks can present checks directly to the paying bank, but this is only practical when a large dollar volume of checks are drawn on a single bank. Otherwise, the cost of transportation outweighs the savings in float and clearing fees paid through direct presentment.

Correspondent banks collect checks for other banks, usually charging a fee for each item cleared. Major check clearing banks can offer highly competitive availability schedules because they have the volume to justify extensive direct presentment programs, sophisticated high-speed processing equipment, and expensive transportation networks that allow them to meet deposit and presentment deadlines throughout the country. Some correspondents offer full-scale nationwide clearing service, while others specialize in clearing items within a particular region.

The Federal Reserve System is the nation's largest clearing agent by a large margin. It is estimated that the Federal Reserve handles between 30 and 40 percent of all checks written in the United States, and that it has better than a 40 percent share of the check collection business. The Federal Reserve presents checks to all paying banks, either directly or through "intercept" banks designated by paying institutions. The Federal Reserve charges a fee for each item cleared, except U.S. Treasury checks and its own checks, which are cleared free of charge. The Federal Reserve offers competitive availability for most checks, with more uniform availability for items drawn on various sized banks within a region than is typically found among correspondents, which frequently offer better availability for high volume points.

Federal Reserve banks clear checks drawn on banks in other regions through the Federal Reserve office or Regional Check Processing Center (RCPC) in that region. In all, there are 48 Federal Reserve check processing sites. Exhibit 5.2 lists Federal Reserve processing centers. For example, the San Francisco Federal Reserve Bank clears checks drawn on banks in South Carolina through the Columbia RCPC of the Charlotte branch of the Richmond Federal Reserve. Banks can collect checks either by depositing them with their local branch, which will clear then through the Federal Reserve system, or by sending them directly to the Federal Reserve office or RCPC for the region on which they are drawn. By

Figure 5.2   Federal Reserve Routing Number Table

Routing Symbols	Description
0110	Boston City
0116, 0117	Northwestern New England RCPC
0113, 0014, 0015	Boston RCPC
0111, 0118, 0119 (0211 paper only)	Windsor Locks RCPC
0112	Lewiston RCPC
0210, 0260	New York City: Delivered to Jericho
(0211 electric only), 0215, 0126	Jericho RCPC
0220	Buffalo City
0223	Buffalo RCPC
0212	Cranford RCPC
0214, 0219, 0280	Jericho RCPC
0213	Utica RCPC
0310, 0360	Philadelphia City
0319, 0311, 0312, 0313	Philadelphia RCPC
0410	Cleveland City
0412	Cleveland RCPC
0420	Cincinnati City
0421, 0422, 0423	Cincinnati RCPC
0430	Pittsburgh City
0432, 0433, 0434	Pittsburgh RCPC
0440	Columbus City
0441, 0442	Columbus RCPC
0510	Richmond City
0514	Richmond RCPC
0520	Baltimore City
0540, 0550, 0560, 0570, 0521, 0522	Baltimore RCPC
0530	Charlotte City
0531	Charlotte RCPC
0539	Columbia City
0532	Columbia RCPC
0519	Charleston City
0515	Charleston RCPC
0610	Atlanta City
0611, 0612, 0613	Atlanta RCPC
0620	Birmingham City
0621, 0622	Birmingham RCPC
0630	Jacksonville City
0631, 0632	Jacksonville RCPC
0640	Nashville City
0641, 0642	Nashville RCPC
0650	New Orleans City
0651, 0652, 0653, 0654, 0655	New Orleans RCPC
0660	Miami City
0670	Miami RCPC
0710	Chicago City
0712, 0719, 0711	Chicago RCPC
0720	Detroit City
0724	Detroit RCPC

Figure 5.2   Federal Reserve Routing Number Table

0730	Des Moines City
0739	Des Moines RCPC
0740	Indianapolis City
0749	Indianapolis RCPC
0750	Milwaukee City
0759	Milwaukee RCPC
0810	St. Louis City
0812, 0815, 0865	St. Louis Country
0819	St. Louis RCPC
0820	Little Rock City
0829	Little Rock RCPC
0830	Louisville City
0813, 0839, 0863	Louisville RCPC
0840	Memphis City
0841, 0842, 0843	Memphis RCPC
0910, 0960	Minneapolis City
0911, 0912, 0913, 0914, 0915	Minneapolis Country
0918, 0919	Minneapolis RCPC
0920	Helena City
0921	Helena Country
0929	Helena RCPC
1010	Kansas City City
1011, 1012, 1019	Kansas City Country
1020	Denver City
1021, 0122, 1023	Denver Country
1070	Denver RCPC
1030	Oklahoma City City
1031	Oklahoma City Country
1039	Oklahoma City RCPC
1040	Omaha City
1041	Omaha Country
1049	Omaha RCPC
1110	Dallas City
1111, 1113	Dallas Country
1119	Dallas RCPC
1120	El Paso City
1122, 1123, 1163	El Paso Country
1130	Houston City
1131	Houston RCPC
1140	San Antonio City
1149	San Antonio RCPC
1210	San Francisco City
1214	San Francisco Country
1211, 1212, 1213	San Francisco RCPC
1220, 1223	Los Angeles City
1221, 1222, 1224	Los Angeles RCPC
1230	Portland City
1231, 1232, 1233	Portland RCPC
1240	Salt Lake City City
1241, 1242, 1243	Salt Lake City RCPC
1250	Seattle City
1251, 1252	Seattle RCPC

sending items directly to the RCPC, banks avoid a transportation surcharge levied by their local Federal Reserve on out-of-district items, and they can often obtain better availability as well.

In the process of collection, a check might be handled by a number of banks. First, of course, is the depositary bank. The depositary bank might then deposit the item with a correspondent bank for collection. The correspondent can clear the check by direct presentment, through a clearinghouse, through the Federal Reserve, or through another correspondent. It is not uncommon for a check to be handled by four or more banks in the clearing process.

Clearing Agent Selection

Correspondent banks and the Federal Reserve offer a bewildering variety of check collection alternatives, providing numerous variations of deadlines, pricing, and availability. For the large volume of checks that are not collected through clearing houses or by direct presentment, careful selection of clearing agents can have a substantial impact on float and clearing costs.

Effective clearing agent selection is based on an understanding of the type of checks to be cleared, of internal check processing schedules, of clearing agent deadlines, of transportation alternatives, and of clearing agent pricing and availability. The unique combination of these factors at each bank results in different optimal selection of clearing agents.

Endpoint Analysis

First, it is essential to know the makeup of the checks to be cleared. This is usually explained by a report called an endpoint analysis. An **endpoint** is the financial institution at which a check is payable and to which it must be presented for collection. Each endpoint is identified by its unique routing number. An endpoint analysis report lists each endpoint, with the number and total dollar value of checks drawn on that point. The report often gives summary totals for groups of endpoints, such as all endpoints in a particular check processing region. An endpoint analysis can cover a day, a month, or some other period, and it might report aggregate or daily

Table 5.1   **Endpoint Analysis**

Endpoint	# Items	Total $ Value
0110-0001	1,023	823,953
0110-0002	983	693,122
0110-0003	1,386	996,203
0100-0006	221	102,990
Total - 0110-XXXX	3,613	2,616,268

average totals for each endpoint. Some banks produce endpoint analyses for different times of the day or for different
days of the week. Table 5.3 shows a typical endpoint analysis.

The endpoint analysis tells what kind of mix and volume
of checks a bank can expect to handle, based on past experience. The analysis should be updated frequently to adjust for
changes in deposited item mix. Most check processing systems are able to produce endpoint analyses on an ongoing
basis. Smaller banks can usually obtain an endpoint analysis
from their primary clearing agent.

Processing Schedules and Workflow Analysis

In addition to knowing what type of checks need to be
cleared, it is important to know when they need to be cleared.
The check clearing alternatives available at noon are much
different than those available at midnight. Clearing schedules are based on the availability of checks after they have
been captured and sorted.

In many banks, checks are available at various times
throughout the day. Processing of lockbox and loan payment
checks might be completed by late morning or early afternoon. Some branch deposits are usually available for processing in the early afternoon, while the bulk of branch work
arrives in the late afternoon to early evening. Large corporate deposits usually arrive in the afternoon or late evening.
Consequently, a large share of deposited checks are processed in the evening, and they are available for dispatch in
cash letters between branch closing time and midnight.

Table 5.2   Distribution of Work to Dispatch Area

Time Period	Work Available		Work Available Cumulative	
	Items	*%*	*Items*	*%*
Before 5:30	0	0	0	0
5:31–6:00	18,000	9	18,000	9
6:01–6:30	18,000	9	36,000	18
6:31–7:00	18,000	9	54,000	27
7:01–7:30	18,000	9	72,000	36
7:31–8:00	18,000	9	90,000	45
8:01–8:30	18,000	9	108,000	54
8:31–9:00	18,000	9	126,000	63
9:01–9:30	18,000	9	144,000	72
9:31–10:00	18,000	9	162,000	81
10:01–10:30	18,000	9	180,000	90
10:31–11:00	18,000	9	198,000	99
11:01–11:30	2,000	1	200,000	100

Correspondent banks that act as clearing agents often receive work throughout the night and early morning hours.

There are two tools that can be used to determine when items are available for cash letters. One tool is an endpoint analysis by time of day, as mentioned earlier. This gives an idea of not only when the work is available, but also of the mix of items throughout the day. Another is a cumulative workflow chart, which shows what percentage of the day's volume is available by each deadline. An example of a cumulative workflow chart is shown in Table 5.2. A cumulative workflow chart is especially useful when projecting the impact of a change in cash letter deadlines.

Although checks are processed in a continuous workflow as the day progresses, banks generally establish one or more transit deadlines for dispatching cash letters. Most mid-sized to large banks have multiple cash letter dispatch deadlines. Checks that meet earlier deadlines usually receive better

Table 5.3   Availability Schedule

LOCATION	ABA NUMBER(S)	AVAILABILITY	DEADLINE Southern California	Northern California
FRB DISTRICT SEVEN				
Chicago				
City	0710	0	8:30 PM	8:00 PM
First National Bank	0710-0001	0	5:00 AM	5:00 AM
Continental Illinois	0710-0003	0	5:00 AM	5:00 AM
Northern Trust	0710-0015	0	5:00 AM	5:00 AM
Harris Trust	0710-0028	0	5:00 AM	5:00 AM
Cole Taylor Bank/Drovers	0710-0034	0	8:30 PM	8:30 PM
LaSalle National Bank	0710-0050	0	8:30 PM	8:30 PM
Boulevard Bank	0710-0052	0	8:30 PM	8:30 PM
Exchange National Bank	0710-0054	0	8:30 PM	8:30 PM
American National Bank	0710-0077	0	5:00 AM	5:00 AM
RCPC	0711, 0712, 0719	1	5:00 AM	5:00 AM
Detroit				
City	0720	0	8:00 PM	7:00 PM
Comerica Bank	0720-0009	0	8:30 PM	7:00 PM
National Bank of Detroit	0720-0032	0	5:00 AM	8:30 PM
Manufacturers National Bank	0720-0033	0	8:30 PM	8:30 PM
Michigan National Bank	0720-0080	0	8:30 PM	8:30 PM
First of America	0720-0091	0	8:30 PM	8:30 PM
RCPC	0724	1	5:00 AM	5:00 AM
Old Kent Bank, Grand Rapids	0724-0005	0	8:30 PM	8:30 PM
Michigan National, Lansing	0724-1174	0	8:30 PM	8:30 PM
Des Moines				
City	0730	0	8:00 PM	7:00 PM
First Interstate Bank of Iowa	0730-0017	0	8:30 PM	8:30 PM
Norwest Bank	0730-0022	0	8:30 PM	8:30 PM
Bankers Trust	0730-0064	0	8:30 PM	8:30 PM
RCPC	0739	1	5:00 AM	5:00 AM
Indianapolis				
City	0740	0	8:00 PM	7:00 PM
Bank One	0740-0001	0	8:30 PM	8:30 PM
Indiana National Bank	0740-0005	0	8:30 PM	7:00 PM
Merchants National Bank	0740-0006	0	8:30 PM	7:00 PM
RCPC	0749	1	5:00 AM	5:00 AM
Milwaukee				
City	0750	0	8:00 PM	7:00 PM
Bank One	0750-0001	0	8:30 PM	8:30 PM
First Wisconsin	0750-0002	0	8:30 PM	8:30 PM
Marshall & Ilsley	0750-0005	0	8:30 PM	8:30 PM
RCPC	0759	1	5:00 AM	5:00 AM

availability than those sent later in the evening, so banks try
to process the largest percentage of the day's work by early
deadlines.

Availability Schedules

Once you know the mix and volume of checks to be
cleared, and the times at which the work is available, it is
time to begin looking at clearing agent availability schedules.
An **availability schedule** is a table published by the clearing agent that advertises the availability of check deposits.
An availability schedule typically lists the float allocated to
check deposits by endpoint and deposit deadlines. Table 5.3 is
an example of an availability schedule.

Based on the time of day work is available for each
endpoint, or on the group of endpoints, the float manager can
determine which clearing agent deadlines the bank can meet.
Be sure to allow time for cash letter preparation in your check
processing shop, as well as time for transportation to the
clearing agent's receiving point. There might be several possible deadlines for each endpoint, each with a different percentage of work processed. Once you have determined the
applicable deadlines, determine the availability for checks on
each endpoint.

Assessing availability can be tricky, because availability
schedules can be difficult to interpret. Different clearing
agents use different formats for their schedules, and some
can be misleading. Most availability schedules, however,
follow general industry practice. Availability is usually expressed as the number of days float assigned to the deposit for
each check. Therefore, "0" indicates same-day availability,
"1" means next day availability, and "2" means two-days
deferred availability. Remember, however, that availability
is based on the date of ledger credit. If a deposit is received
after the ledger deadline, it will be posted on the following
day. In addition, availability is usually stated as-of a cash
letter deadline, after which an additional day of float is
added. Deadlines are usually local time for the clearing
agent.

For example, an availability schedule might list the following availability:

Table 5.4   Availability: Philadelphia—City

Endpoint	Availability	Cash Letter Deadline (1)
0310-XXXX	0	11:30 P.M.

(1)   Ledger Deadline: 6:00 P.M.

If a bank deposits checks drawn on a Philadelphia bank (routing numbers beginning with 0310) at 10:00 P.M., it will receive availability the following business day. It receives same-day availability, but the deposit is not credited until the next day because it was received after the 6:00 P.M. ledger cutoff. If the deposit was made at midnight, availability would be deferred an additional day because the deposit was received after the 11:30 P.M. cash letter deadline.

Availability schedules usually list availability for groups of endpoints, such as all endpoints in a city or RCPC territory. The schedule might then list individual endpoints within the group that receive better availability, have different deadlines, or have special pricing. These are usually endpoints to which the clearing agent sends checks for direct presentment.

A complication in determining availability for deposited checks is the practice of allocating fractional float. The Federal Reserve Banks, as well as a number of correspondent banks, charge float back to depositors for delays in collecting checks due to such factors as bad weather and transportation problems. This is usually accomplished by deferring availability on a fraction of each deposit to make up for the clearing agent's lost availability due to missed deadlines. The net result of fractional float allocation is an increase in clearing time for each endpoint. If possible, the effect of fractional float should be included when determining endpoint availability. Be sure to understand the clearing agent's policy on assessing fractional float, the method of calculation, and both historical and projected assessment factors.

Some clearing agents offer better availability or deadlines for checks over a certain dollar amount. An example is the High Dollar Group Sort program of the Federal Reserve, and similar programs are offered by major correspondent banks. There is usually a higher fee for clearing these items and receiving enhanced availability. Clearing agents sometimes offer later deadlines or lower fees for checks sorted by endpoint, or by endpoint groups. The Federal Reserve offers such options through its Fine Sort and Group Sort programs. Again, correspondents frequently have similar offerings.

Clearing agents sometimes include clearing fees on their availability schedules, but more often, prices are published on a separate schedule. The Federal Reserve and most correspondents charge a per-item fee for each check cleared. There are often different fees for different types of checks. For example, a correspondent bank might charge a lower price for checks drawn on banks in its own local clearing house. Other charges include cash letter or deposit fees, wire transfer fees to draw down funds, and other miscellaneous fees.

When analyzing clearing agent alternatives, be sure to look at what a variety of correspondent banks have to offer, as well as at the schedules for the local Federal Reserve and RCPCs throughout the country. It is likely that the optimum selection will include cash letter sends to a number of correspondent banks, the local Federal Reserve, and several RCPCs.

Transportation

One more factor plays an important role in selecting clearing agents: the availability and cost of transportation. A clearing agent might offer excellent availability and pricing, but if there is no way of delivering the checks before deadline, or if doing so is prohibitively expensive, it is not a viable alternative.

Cash letters must be transported rapidly to obtain good availability. For local checks or items sent to nearby cities, ground couriers are usually adequate. Because a large share of checks handled by banks are typically drawn on nearby banks, a substantial volume of items travel overland. But for checks going outside a relatively limited area, ground transport is simply too slow. Interdistrict checks generally go by air.

One option is the package service offered by most commercial airlines on regularly scheduled flights. Checks are delivered airport-to-airport within hours. This service is particularly appropriate for cash letters dispatched during the day or early evening, when most commercial flights are scheduled.

But flights are subject to the same delays that affect commercial passengers, and the bank often must arrange transportation from the destination airport to the clearing agent's processing center.

Most checks are transported in the late evening, too late for scheduled commercial flights. Banks, therefore, charter flights to high-volume points for check clearings. Often, several banks will share the cost of a charter flight. Charter rates are often reasonable in the evening because demand from other users is lower than in the daytime.

In the mid-1980s, a number of specialized air carriers began offering low-cost cash letter transport services to major cities and Federal Reserve RCPCs. For a reasonable charge per package, these carriers pick up cash letters at sites throughout the country, fly them to a hub, sort them by destination, and fly them to correspondent banks and Federal Reserve offices. Many of the air couriers have teamed with ground couriers to provide door-to-door service.

In the early 1980s, First Tennessee Bank teamed with Federal Express, the overnight package service, to create a check collection service that combines check clearing with transportation. For a per-item fee, the service, called First Express, picks up cash letters from airports throughout the country and ships them on regular Federal Express package flights to Memphis, Tennessee, the location of both the Federal Express hub and First Tennessee's check processing operation.

The Federal Reserve offers a similar service through its Interdistrict Transportation System (ITS). ITS is the network of couriers used by the Federal Reserve for its own interdistrict clearings, but in the mid-1980s, transportation was unbundled as a separate service for banks sending checks to other Federal Reserve districts and RCPCs. Check packages are delivered to the nearest Federal Reserve processing location, which forwards them through the ITS. The Federal Reserve levies a per-item transportation surcharge in addition to the clearing fee charged at the destination.

Clearing Agent Analysis

Armed with endpoint analyses, availability schedules, and courier timetables, next analyze clearing alternatives.

There are four main criteria for selecting clearing agents: availability, clearing fees, transportation costs and other operating costs. Determining the optimal combination of clearing agents requires a deft balancing of these factors.

It is unlikely that you will find a single clearing agent offering the best availability, lowest per-item prices, cheapest transportation, and best negligible miscellaneous expense to clear every endpoint. In fact, it is doubtful you will find such a combination for more than a handful of endpoints, if at all. Instead, clearing agent selection is the result of trade-offs. Better availability usually costs more in clearing fees,, transportation costs, or both.

You can compare clearing agents by calculating the fee equivalent of additional float. First, determine the average value of each check for the selected endpoint. Then multiply the average check dollar value by the opportunity investment rate used to value float reduction benefits. Divide this amount by 365 to determine the daily float cost, then multiply the daily cost by the number of days increase in float. Finally, reduce this figure by the required reserve rate to determine the daily cost of float, net of reserves. The equation is expressed as follows:

[Average Check x Investment Rate x Days Float x (1 - Reserve %)] ÷ 365 Days in a Year = Fee Equivalent

For example, if one clearing agent offers one-day availability for an endpoint, another offers two-day availability, and the average check value is $450, the fee equivalent of the difference in float 8.7 cents assuming an 8 percent opportunity investment rate and a 12 percent reserve requirement:

$$\frac{\$450 \times 8\% \times 1}{365} \times (1 - 12\%) = 8.7 \text{ cents}$$

All things being equal, the value of clearing checks one day faster is worth 8.7 cents per item in additional clearing fees, transportation costs and other expenses. Conversely, for an 8.7 cent per item difference in costs, the break-even point for float reduction is $450 dollars per item. In other words, if a check is for an amount of $450 or more, it is worth paying up to 8.7 cents in extra costs to clear the item one-day faster.

The logic behind this float break-even analysis is the basis for dollar-cutoff endpoint sorting. Checks greater than the cutoff amount are sent to the clearing agent offering better availability for a higher price, while those under the cutoff are sent to the cheaper alternative offering poorer availability.

Before selecting clearing agents, other factors besides a simple calculation of availability versus clearing costs should be considered. As discussed earlier, much of the float savings may be passed on to customers in the form of improved availability. It is also unlikely that the cash letter will always arrive as scheduled, so it is important to project for missed deadlines. The courier's record for reliability, as well as historical weather conditions for the origin and destination airports, are predictors of future deadline performance.

Another factor that complicates the analysis of clearing alternatives is the way checks on different endpoints are grouped together for cash letters. There are also fixed costs for sending a package to each **sendpoint** (cash letter destination). One fixed cost is the cost of transportation. It usually costs the same to send a thousand checks or one check in a package, so the cost per-item of transportation declines as more checks are included in a cash letter. Other costs, such as deposit fees, are also charged on a cash letter basis.

A somewhat intangible factor in selecting clearing agents is the complexity of the check collection program. As the number of sendpoints increases, so does the number of sorter repasses and the difficulty of preparing cash letters for each transit deadline. The more complicated the check clearing operation, the greater the likelihood of making mistakes. If adding sendpoints requires adding staff for cash letter preparation and dispatch, this is a cost that must be included in the analysis.

In addition, it is important to understand how the bank will compensate the clearing agent for its services. The Federal Reserve, for example, deducts fees directly from reserve account balances. Correspondent banks are paid either in fees or through account analysis. If the bank will be paying with compensating balances through account analysis, it is important to adjust published fees to allow for differences between the earnings credit rate (ECR) used by the correspondent and the opportunity investment rate for due-from balances.

The earnings credit rate offered by clearing agent banks is often lower than the rate a bank could earn through alternative investments. If, for example, the correspondent's ECR is 6.5 percent, and the bank could earn 7.5 percent in the Fed Funds market, the effect is that compensating balances incur a 1 percent interest penalty, increasing the effective cost of the correspondent bank's services. Banks normally adjust compensating balances for reserve requirements, which will further dilute the value of balances held to pay for services.

An exception is balances held in a clearing account at the Federal Reserve to pay for check fees. Clearing account balances are held separate from reserve account balances, and they earn credit toward fees at the average Fed Funds rate. Furthermore, there is no adjustment for reserves, meaning all of the money is applied as compensating balances. Clearing account balances can also be used to cover debits against the reserve account, reducing the potential for overdraft and simplifying funds management.

A final factor that must be considered in evaluating check collection options is the depository risk of the clearing bank. The Federal Deposit Insurance Corporation insures deposits up to $100,000, but cash letters can be worth many times this amount. Your bank's credit evaluation of a prospective clearing agent may disqualify it as a depository bank, in which case it cannot be used.

After comparing availability, clearing fees, transportation costs and all the other factors, your goal is to arrive at an optimal selection of clearing agents. Some banks may only need a few clearing agents, while others may send hundreds of cash letters a day. It all depends on the mix and volume of checks, the sophistication of the check processing operation, the availability of transportation, and the offerings of clearing agents.

Clearing Models

As you can see, analysis of clearing agents can be a complex undertaking. For most mid-sized and larger banks, it is impossible to analyze all clearing options simultaneously using conventional pencil-and-paper methods. Instead, banks have tended to analyze incremental improvements over current sending patterns for a limited number of endpoints at a time.

A popular alternative method of clearing agent analysis involves the use of computer models. A number of software vendors license mainframe and personal computer systems that are capable of analyzing large numbers of clearing alternatives for a full range of endpoints. Clearing models generally are bundled with a subscription service that supplies and updates computer formatted availability and pricing schedules for various clearing agents. The systems can usually be linked to the endpoint analysis system for ongoing updates. In fact, clearing models have been integrated into the check processing systems of several large banks, allowing adjustments in cash letter sendings based on the mix of work in process.

Direct Presentment

As mentioned earlier, direct presentment is an alternative to using clearing agents that is often viable for high-volume points. Most cash letters to correspondent banks include some items drawn on that bank. But there are also endpoints that represent large enough volumes alone to justify the transportation expense required for direct presentment. These include banks that are simply so large that their customer bases generate lots of checks, cash management controlled disbursement banks, and banks that specialize in niche check products such as rebate checks or insurance drafts, among others.

In order to present checks directly to the paying bank, it is necessary to arrange for transportation and settlement. Transportation alternatives are the same as for any other clearing alternative. Settlement, however, can be trickier. You may wish to open a correspondent account with the paying bank, or arrange for a daily wire transfer of funds.

Some banks charge presentment fees, often as a way of discouraging direct sends for same day credit. As with any other cost, presentment fees must be balanced against float savings when evaluating the benefit of direct presentment.

Whenever an endpoint is selected for direct presentment,

it is important to reanalyze sendings to the clearing agent that had previously collected the items. Because direct presentment endpoints generally represent high check volumes, pulling these checks out of a cash letter can have a substantial impact on the viability of the clearing agent for the remaining items.

Workflow Management

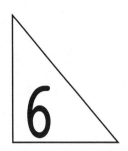

Check clearing optimization is an effective technique for reducing the check float that banks incur in the course of doing business. But clearing optimization alone is limited by the flow of checks through item processing; attractive clearing alternatives are often passed over because checks are simply not ready to send in time for cash letter deadlines.

Float managers can play a more active role in float reduction by working with check processing managers to improve the flow of work through item processing operations. The benefits of improved workflow, combined with check collection adjustments that capitalize on the ability to meet new deadlines, can be substantial, and they can far exceed the value of clearing optimization alone.

The flow of checks through a bank from the point of receipt to the point of collection is a key determinant of a bank's total float and profitability. The ability of management to optimize the check processing environment is based on the ability to understand the true cost of each production component, and to understand how the cost of each component will vary with changes in the production environment. Float is one of the major costs associated with check processing operations, but its role as a production cost component is often overlooked.

It is difficult to cost justify a labor saving machine if one does not understand labor costs, or how one's labor costs vary with changes in staffing levels. Likewise, it is difficult to cost justify equipment designed to facilitate the smooth flow of checks and thus reduce float if one does not understand the cost of float or how float costs vary with changes in workflow. While it is ludicrous to assume that a production manager does not understand labor costs and how labor costs will vary changes in staffing levels, the sad fact is that many otherwise competent production managers possess only a rudimentary understanding of the cost of float.

The Role of the Float Manager

Managing the flow of checks through the bank is not the responsibility of the float manager. Managing the flow of checks through the bank is best left to production managers and line managers in item processing. But this does not mean the float manager should not play a role in workflow management.

While the responsibility of the float manager varies, in most banks he or she is responsible for designing the bank's check clearing network. The float manager will choose the clearing agents, schedule transportation for cash letter sends, and establish cash letter dispatch deadlines. The production manager is charged with the responsibility of meeting transit deadlines.

In some banks, there is a single transit deadline. Understanding the cost of missing this deadline is rather simple. In other banks, there are multiple dispatch deadlines. Understanding the cost of missing any one of these deadlines can be quite complicated. Each check processed by the bank will have one deadline at which an additional day of float is incurred. Most items will also have a deadline at which the clearing fee paid to collect the check will increase. Frequently, the clearing fee deadlines differ from the availability deadlines, and some items can have multiple clearing fee deadlines.

The role the float manager plays in workflow management is one of assisting the production manager in identifying the real costs associated with clearing an item after its optimum deadline. This task increases in complexity as the number of clearing deadlines increases for the bank.

Understanding the Costs of Missed Deadlines

The float manager can help the production manager optimize the check clearing function by associating costs with each missed deadline. To illustrate, let us assume the following processing environment in Table 6.1.

Table 6.1 Processing Environment

Daily Processing Statistics

Daily production volume	200,000 items
Proof Machines	20 machines
Proof operators	20 operators
Paid hours per day	6 hrs.
Average item size	$1000

Daily Cost Statistics

Item	*Cost Per Item*
Encoding Personnel	$0.010
Encoding Equipment	0.005
Management and Equipment	0.005
Total Cost Per Item	$0.020

Distribution of Work to Dispatch Area

Time Period	*Work Available*		*Work Available Cumulative*	
	Items	*%*	*Items*	*%*
Before 5:30	0	0	0	0
5:31-6:00	18,000	9	18,000	9
6:01-6:30	18,000	9	36,000	18
6:31-7:00	18,000	9	54,000	27
7:01-7:30	18,000	9	72,000	36
7:31-8:00	18,000	9	90,000	45
8:01-8:30	18,000	9	108,000	54
8:31-9:00	18,000	9	126,000	63
9:01-9:30	18,000	9	144,000	72
9:31-10:00	18,000	9	162,000	81
10:01-10:30	18,000	9	180,000	90
10:31-11:00	18,000	9	198,000	99
11:01-11:30	2,000	1	200,000	100

Table 6.1 *continued*

Key Deadlines			
Deadline	*Type of Work*	*Impact*	*Work Affected*
8:30 P.M.	Selected out of District RCPC	$0.02 increase in clearing fee	2%
9:00 P.M.	Selected out of District City	$0.03 decrease in clearing fee, 1 day increase in float	8%
10:00 P.M.	Selected High Dollar Group Sort	$0.02 decrease clearing fees, 1 day increase in float	10%
12:00 P.M.	All other points		

In Table 6.1, the production manager is proud of the check processing operation. In the past year, the proof department stopped employing full-time proof encoders and now uses part-time or modified shift employees. While this requires more machines and a higher hourly salary rate, these costs were offset by reduced benefits expense and higher encoding productivity. The move to part-time encoding staff also allowed an earlier proof close-out time, reducing float and allowing the branches to receive morning reports before opening. The manager production is quite proud of the department's workflow.

In discussions with the float manager, the production manager resisted proposals for further improvements in workflow through proof for the following reasons:

- 95% of all items processed Monday through Thursday currently obtained the best availability of the day, with 100% of items processed on Friday receiving the best availability.

- To speed up the delivery of work to cash letter dispatch by 30 minutes would increase encoding costs by 7.5 percent, and to expedite workflow by one hour would increase encoding costs by 12 percent.

- Improving workflow by 30 minutes or one hour would only result in 1.62 percent or 3.24 percent of the day's work being cleared earlier, and this would be at least partly offset by increased clearing fees.

Despite the production manager's concerns, the float manager was able to show the benefits of improved workflow in the following cost/benefit analysis in Table 6.2.

Table 6.2   Annual Cost/Benefit Analysis

Costs	30 minute Improvement in workflow	One hour Improvement in workflow
Increased encoding costs	$75,000	$120,000
Increased clearing fees		
City points	8,640	17,280
High Dollar Group Sort	7,200	14,400
Annual Increased Costs	$90,840	$151,680
Benefits		
Reduced clearing fees on out-of-district RCPC	$1,440	$2,880
Float savings on City endpoints @ 8 %	57,929	151,858
Float savings on HDGS endpoints @ 8 %	72,411	144,822
Annual Benefit	$131,780	$263,560
Net Annual Benefit	$40,940	$111,880

Despite some reasonable indications that an improvement in work flow would yield little if any savings, the float manager was able to show a substantial benefit associated with fine tuning the production workflow.

Ways to Improve Workflow

There are a number of ways to expedite the flow of checks through item processing operations. Most are outside the control of the float manager, but the float manager can help implement these improvements by identifying and explaining the benefits to production and line managers.

Inbound Transportation

One of the most common problems in workflow management is uneven arrival of branch work in the proof department. At a typical bank, most work arrives from the branches late in the afternoon or early in the evening, although some is delivered much earlier. Proof managers are reluctant to bring in encoding staff to handle the early work because after it is encoded the operators wait idle until the bulk of the branch deliveries arrive. Instead, they wait until a backlog has developed, and then they bring in enough encoders to work off the backlog by closeout.

Even though branch deliveries tend to arrive late in the day, much of the work is available in the branches much earlier. In fact, a large portion of the work comprises morning deposits by businesses that are made before noon. If these items can be picked up from the branches and delivered to proof throughout the day, there will be enough work available to justify an earlier start for at least part of the proof encoding staff. The net result would be that a larger percentage of checks would meet early cash letter deadlines.

There are two factors that affect the delivery of branch work to proof. One is courier schedules. More courier pickups would need to be scheduled earlier in the day, and this could increase transportation costs. The increase in cost would need to be weighed against the check clearing benefit.

The other is teller procedures. Tellers are frequently reluctant to release work early in the day, because they want to have deposits available to aid in balancing at the end of the day. Teller balancing policies might need to be adjusted to counter resistance to early release of work.

Proof Staffing

Proof encoding labor is often the largest single cost of check processing. Proof managers are understandably reluctant to increase the number of proof operators to expedite workflow. One of the difficulties in managing proof staffing levels is that workflow can be erratic, varying substantially from one night to the next, and usually arriving in bulk at the end of the day.

Proof staffing can be matched to workflow better if the department employs part-time and flexible shift operators. More operators, working fewer hours per night, can encode the same amount of work in a shorter time. Historical tracking of encoding volume can also help, by helping predict peak volume days.

Proof Productivity

Incentive programs, training, and procedural changes that improve proof productivity can have an obvious positive effect on staffing costs, but they can also yield float benefits. Float benefits occur because improvements in proof productivity are also increased in proof throughput. If productivity increases from 1,200 items per hour to 1,400 items per hour, 200 more items per hour will meet earlier deadlines.

Transit Operations

Delays and bottlenecks in the flow of work from proof, through the reader/sorters, to cash letter dispatch, and out the door reduce the percentage of checks meeting early transit deadlines. The entire operation should be analyzed thoroughly to identify procedures that impede workflow unnecessarily.

The Float Hunt 7

Most bank float is associated with the collection of deposited checks. Therefore, most float management efforts are directed toward reducing check collection float through clearing optimization and workflow improvement or allocation of float to depository customers. But float management is not simply a check collection function. A lot of float can be found outside of check processing—you just need to find it.

Looking for float is in many ways like going on a safari; in this case, it's a float hunt. The terrain is often unfamiliar, ranging through virtually every department of the bank. The prey is frequently camouflaged or hidden, unseen by the casual observer. Many will even deny that it even exists. Therefore, the skilled float hunter must stalk his quarry by following a trail of telltale entries to suspense accounts.

Float is a creature of the balance sheet, so the map for the float hunt is a general-ledger account report. Any account with unexplained debit balances should be explored to see if they represent sterile funds.

The prize in this quest can be substantial. Significant sums of float often can be eliminated through simple procedural changes. Other float can be allocated once it is identified. In most cases, float savings come from areas that never would have been affected by traditional approaches to check collection float management. In addition, because much of this "miscellaneous" float results from internal inefficiencies, there are frequently nonfloat benefits associated with the improvements as well.

Float management is a creative discipline. Float managers are constantly finding new opportunities for float reduction, sometimes in unexpected areas. The following examples of float can be found in many banks. But don't be limited by this list—the creative float hunter should be able to find opportunities where others have not looked before.

Dialing for Dollars

Murphy's Law states that, "If something can go wrong, it will go wrong." Everyone is familiar with this phenomenon, particularly the transit manager. Cash letters set to be delivered to paying banks or clearing banks a few minutes before deadline are often delivered a few minutes after the deadline. Late delivery of items results in additional float, usually referred to as "missed deadlines float."

Missed deadlines float will frequently average approximately 5 percent of out-of-district transit totals. Consequently, the cost of missed deadlines float can be very significant. Most banks attempt to manage missed deadlines float by managing the couriers who deliver the cash letters. This approach is necessary and can be quite effective. Some banks, however, have taken the additional step of instituting a "Dialing for Dollars" program.

"Dialing for Dollars" involves personal contact, via telephone, between the sending bank and the check clearing bank. The program is designed to reduce missed deadlines float dramatically. Three different approaches are employed. The first approach is to validate that a cash letter was in fact delivered before the appropriate deadline, not after. Banks make mistakes, and big check clearing banks tend to make lots of mistakes. If your cash letter was received and time-stamped before the deadline, cash letter credit should not be deferred. Bringing this matter to the attention of your clearing bank will normally resolve the matter.

The second approach is to ask for leniency. If you have reason to believe that your cash letter will be delivered late, call your clearing bank and ask that it hold its window open for your cash letter. Transit managers, particularly those who work the night shifts, are generally very understanding and easy to work with, as they have not been educated in the arrogant indifference of daytime management. A simple request to provide special handling for late work can frequently be accomodated.

The third approach is to whine. If my children have taught me anything, it is to never underestimate the power of the whiney, squeaking wheel. A little, "Oh, come on, I didn't miss the deadline by much ... Can't you give me credit this one time?" can go a long way toward reducing missed deadline float. It is easy to forget the lesson we learned while we were dating: You don't get the sale unless you ask for the business.

ACH Posting

Automated Clearing House (ACH) payments are a type of electronic funds transfer handled by banks for their customers. The ACH system is used for such payments as payroll Direct Deposit, corporate cash concentration, recurring consumer bill payments; and more recently, corporate tax and trade payments. Banks can initiate ACH credit transfers for their customers, which move funds out of the originating bank, or ACH debits, which draw funds from another bank. Banks also receive ACH debits and credits for their customers, posting the entries accordingly.

A bank originating ACH transactions creates a file that is sent to the regional ACH processor for clearing. Transactions are dated for settlement one or more days after delivery to the processor. The transactions are then routed to receiving banks for delivery that evening or the following day.

ACH rules require banks to make funds for Direct Deposit available to recipients at the start of business on settlement date. Because most banks update account information in the evening, a credit posted in the morning does not affect the ledger balance until after the close of business. In order to comply with ACH rules, many banks post ACH credits the day before settlement date. Because the bank does not receive funds until settlement, it incurs one day of float by posting credits early.

Banks also incur float when they post ACH debits originated by customers on creation date instead of settlement date. An ACH debit is actually a credit to the originator because it draws funds from another bank. Banks sometimes post ACH debit originations as customer deposits, with one-day assignment of float. In both instances, float can be eliminated by waiting to post transactions on settlement date. Doing so, however, will probably require system or operational modifications.

The bank must be able to give customers early morning availability of Direct Deposit funds before posting the ledger credit. The most common way to accomplish this is through a process called "memo posting." On-line systems, such as teller terminals and ATMs, show the increase in a customer's available balance, but the actual ledger balance is not affected until later in the evening. This is the same type of treatment that allows cash deposits and wire transfers to be credited to customer's accounts for immediate withdrawal.

Posting ACH debit originations requires operational or system changes that separate processing of ACH files from the posting of entries. This is usually accomplished by holding transactions in a file until settlement date, which is a process called "warehousing." Most current versions of ACH software offer this capability.

Cash Concentration

Many banks offer cash concentration services to cash management customers using depository transfer checks (DTCs) or through the ACH. Cash concentration is designed for corporations with many retail outlets scattered over a broad geographical area. For various reasons, these retail stores usually cannot deposit daily receipts into the same bank. For example, the retail stores may be in different states or in unit banking states. The corporate cash manager must consolidate or concentrate individual store receipts into one account at one bank for disbursement or investment purposes. Cash concentration is designed to meet these needs.

With the cash concentration service, each retail store reports the day's deposit total to the concentrating bank. The concentrating bank then draws a depository transfer check (DTC) against each retail outlet's depository account for the day's deposit total and deposits all of the DTCs into the concentration account. The DTCs normally clear in one day, about the same time the deposited funds become available at the retail store's depository banks. The same process can work using ACH items instead of DTCs. The service is a relatively inexpensive way to consolidate receipts from multiple locations.

Some banks post cash concentration items on the business day on which they are created and enter the collection stream. The items normally carry one day float (ACH debits are always one day items). Other banks post cash concentration items on the business day following the day on which they are created and enter the collection stream. Under this scenario, the items are posted with no float. This process is referred to as **deferred cash concentration.**

Deferred cash concentration shrinks the bank's balance sheet without changing the bank's earning capacity. As a result, the bank's capital requirements are reduced and return on assets and return on equity ratios are improved. For most banks, these are important consideration in today's environment.

Deferred cash concentration requires the ability to perform two operational tasks. First, the operations area must be able to separate processing and clearing of items from the posting of deposits. The goal is to defer the posting of the customer deposit, not to defer the collection of the item. The second operational task is to provide the cash concentration customer information regarding the total amount of the deferred deposit and the dollar amount that can be withdrawn on the date of posting. If cash concentration customers normally receive available balance information via prior day balance reporting, deferred posting might require a move to same-day reporting, or the prior-day reporting system might need to be altered to accommodate the information.

The benefits associated with reducing assets and reducing capital requirements through deferred cash concentration are a function of cash concentration dollar volume and the value a bank places on the cost of capital. The float manager can check the average cash concentration clearing totals to determine the projected benefit to the bank.

Post All Debits

No float is created when paid items are posted against customer accounts on the date the bank pays for the items. Payor bank float is created when the bank is unable to post items against customers' accounts. As a result, the bank has overstated the customers' actual account balances, which for certain customers will result in reduced bank income.

Many banks do not post checks presented against insufficient funds (NSF checks) to customers' accounts until a decision is made to pay or return the items. Consequently, NSF items, items which if posted would overdraw customers accounts, are not posted on the day the bank pays for the item, but reside in an unposted suspense account until the following day when they are either paid or returned.

The practice of not posting insufficient items originated when posting systems could not easily separate the handling of paper items from the processing of data. In this environment, handling insufficient items as unposted items was significantly less expensive and simpler than returning a posted item, because posted items were not outsorted for special handling. The practice of not posting insufficient items was also established when float was not considered to be a significant operating cost. Today, however, most posting systems will allow both posted and unposted items to be outsorted for special handling.

Posting insufficient items against a customer's account instead of holding them in an unposted account lowers the customer's account balance. To the extent that customer account balances are an important element in determining service charges and account analysis compensation, the practice of posting insufficient items will increase bank earnings. Care should be taken to understand any resulting increase in operating costs and any resulting change in the bank's ability to return an insufficient items.

The float manager can check the balance in the unposted DDA account to determine the approximate value of posting NSF checks. The unposted DDA account will normally contain more than simply unposted NSF items, but the other types of items also present float management opportunities. Any resulting benefits will be due to float allocation and will thus rely on changes in service charges or customer behavior resulting from changes in the customer's reported account balance.

Stop Payment

Another reason that checks fail to post against customer accounts is stop payment orders. A single stop payment order will often cause several checks for the same amount to go unposted and be held for manual review the next day. All except the targeted item will be posted the following day, but the bank incurs float on all the items.

Some banks have chosen to allocate the cost of stop payment float to the customer issuing the order. Allocating stop payment float to the customer can be accomplished by posting the stop payment and stop payment suspects to the customer's account, rather than to the unposted DDA account.

Many banks post stop payment suspects but do not choose to post stop payment. The reasoning is that the cost of unposted float is paid for by the stop payment fee. Some of these banks will increase the cost of a stop payment for items in excess of $10,000 to offset the additional float cost.

Unposted Debits

Some items cannot post to a customer's account. "Account closed" and "Invalid Account Number" are two common reasons. Such unposted items must be researched and resolved. Resolution involves returning the item in the case of a closed account or posting the item to the proper account in the case of an invalid account number. In both cases, the bank incurs the cost of payor bank float. In the case of check drawn on a closed account, there is no customer to absorb the cost of the unposted float. In the case of the invalid account number, when the correct customer is identified, the cost of unposted float can be allocated to the appropriate account.

Allocating unposted float to the proper customer can be accomplished by adjusting the customer's account balance. The customer's account balance is lowered to reflect the fact that a debit was posted to the customer's account on a one-day delayed basis. Some banks automate this adjustment process.

When unposted items are resolved by posting the item to the proper account, most banks post the item under a separate transaction code that force posts the item. The posting system can be designed to create a one-day account balance adjustment for each force posted transaction. This process will allow the customer, rather than the bank, to bear the float costs associated with unposted items.

Suspense Accounts

Most checks are processed within the one day time-frame of standard operating and clearing schedules. A few items, however, are delayed in processing or for some other reason cannot be resolved by the end of the processing day. These items are usually accounted for in suspense accounts until they can be dispatched or cleared.

Suspense balances represent float. Suspense account debits are typically cleared by debiting a customer's account. In these cases, customers enjoyed the use of funds while the bank processed the debits. In essence, the bank gave the customer a short-term loan and received no compensation.

Suspense account credits are the opposite. Credit items are normally cleared by crediting a customer's account. In these cases, the bank has received funds that have not been passed to the appropriate customer. Many banks, for obvious reasons, focus more attention on clearing debit balance suspense items. Likewise, most customers tend to mention missing credits sooner than they mention over-credits or missing debits; such is the nature of life.

The cost of carrying debit balance suspense accounts is a cost associated with the depository function. There are several ways in which banks deal with this cost element. One way is to offset the costs associated with carrying debit balance suspense accounts with the revenue associated with carrying credit balance suspense accounts. With proper focus, a bank can maintain a larger dollar amount of credit balance suspense, thus allowing a complete offset of associated debit expenses. Under this approach, care should be taken not to count credit balance suspense balances that are cleared with both a credit to the customer's account and a back-valued customer balance adjustment. Back-valuing the customer's credit allows the customer to use the back-valued balances to pay the bank for services provided.

A second way to view the costs of carrying debit balance suspense accounts is to recognize the carrying costs as a cost element separate from the revenues associated with credit balance suspense accounts. Under this approach, the carrying cost can be absorbed by the depository products, by reducing product contribution, or the costs can be passed on through a fee or by an increased float allocation charge.

Banks choosing to allocate the costs of carrying debit balance suspense accounts to depositing customers via an increased float allocation will usually take one of two approaches. First, when a customer is debited for an adjustment, the customer also receives a back-valued debit adjustment that decreases the customer's average collected balance. For example, a customer may receive credit for a $100 missing item (i.e., Listed, not Enclosed), and the bank carries a debit balance adjustment for three days before correcting the customer's account. In this case, the bank may adjust the customer's account analysis calculation by lowering the average collected balance by the equivalent of $100 for three days. Most banks will only make these types of adjustments when the amounts involved are significant.

In addition to back-valuing debit balance adjustments, some banks allocate the carrying costs of debit balance suspense accounts to the depositing customers via fractional float assignment. For example, if the average balance of credit balance suspense accounts is about 1% of total average clearings, a bank may assign 1.01 days of float rather than 1 day, and 2.01 days of float rather than 2 days. Under this approach, every depositing customer carries a portion of the costs associated with carrying debit balance suspense accounts.

The benefits associated with passing back-valued adjustments or allocating suspense float to depositing customers is a function of the size of the adjustments, and the effect on customer behavior of changes in collected balances.

In addition to check processing suspense accounts, nearly every other bank department has suspense accounts for items that cannot be cleared or applied by the end of the processing day. Examples of suspense accounts that often carry high balances are those for securities safekeeping, trust, mortgage loan processing, sales finance, and credit card processing.

Loan Operations

Loan payments are second only to deposits as a source of float in banks. Failure to process and clear loan payment checks quickly can increase the float associated with lending.

One way to expedite the clearing of loan checks is to

handle payments using lockbox procedures. Lockbox processing can reduce mail float by using unique ZIP codes and post office boxes, with frequent mail pick-up from the post office throughout the early morning. Processing float is minimized by the use of a streamlined, multi-shift processing environment. **Lockboxes** are generally designed to process the check for immediate clearing by separating the items from accompanying payment coupons used to post loan payments. Check collection float is reduced because the check is ready for clearing early in the processing day, and it is therefore able to meet earlier deadlines for check clearing and presentment.

Even if the loan processing operation cannot be configured for lockbox processing, payment checks can still be released for early clearing. The check can be replaced by a photocopy if it is essential for loan processing. Any float reduction achieved in loan processing increases investable funds, because loan accounts are usually credited for payment upon receipt of the check, not when it clears.

Direct Deposit

As explained earlier, float allocation to consumer accounts is usually only marginally effective at influencing deposit and withdrawal patterns. The largest source of float in most consumer accounts is paycheck deposits. So eliminating the float associated with payroll deposits would be an excellent way to manage float that resists traditional approaches.

Encouraging Direct Deposit of payrolls by ACH is an effective way to reduce the float in consumer accounts. If a customer receives his or her salary through the ACH, the bank receives investable funds on payday, instead of having to clear a paycheck. An added benefit is that receiving an ACH payment is usually much less expensive than processing and clearing a check deposit.

Promotion of Direct Deposit is not a function of float management. It typically falls under the marketing or retail banking division at most banks. But the float manager can assist in the creation of a Direct Deposit program by quantifying the value of float reduction for use in cost/benefit analysis.

Treasury Tax and Loan

Companies pay federal taxes, including employee with-holding taxes, by depositing the funds with banks. Funds are deposited into the Treasury Tax and Loan (TT&L) account, and they are subsequently remitted to the U.S. Treasury. TT&L deposits generally stay in the bank one day. The value of the funds compensates the bank for serving as a Federal depository. The value of TT&L funds is diminished, however, if the deposit is made with a transit check. Banks should, therefore, accept only on-us checks for TT&L deposits. The best way of monitoring compliance with a policy of accepting only on-us items for TT&L is to monitor the ledger and collected balance in the account. Any uncollected funds represent transit items accepted for TT&L deposits, and they should be investigated.

Payable-through Drafts

A payable-through draft is an item that is similar to a check, but which is not paid by the bank until instructed to do so by the drawer. In the strictest sense, the bank is not the payor of the draft, but acts as an agent for the company that issued the item. The issuer may pay or dishonor the draft for whatever reason it chooses.

Payable-through drafts were once more common than they are today, especially for payment of insurance claims. But processing payable-through items is costly, so most have been replaced by controlled disbursement. Most banks still, however, have some payable-through draft customers.

Payable-through drafts frequently are handled as exception items that do not post to demand deposit accounts. This is to allow separate handling of the drafts while the customer is notified and approval is obtained to pay or return the items. The total amount of drafts paid is then debited from the customer's account or funded by a wire transfer. Because there is usually a one day delay between receipt of the items and final payment, the bank incurs one day of float.

This float should be allocated to the customer through account analysis. Because payable-through customers are typically quite cash management conscious, this can be a very effective way of recovering float.

Redeposited Returned Items

Many items returned for insufficient funds will clear if represented a day or two later. This is because a significant percentage of bad checks are written by companies or individuals in anticipation of future deposits. The check writer was hoping to take advantage of float, but underestimated the duration of the float cycle. Depository banks will frequently reclear items returned unpaid instead of charging them back to their customers; this process is called **redepositing**.

In most cases, however, the item is not really redeposited into the customer's account. Instead, it is simply sent back into the collection stream. Because the check does not go through the normal deposit processing cycle, the float associated with reclearing is not allocated to the customer.

Banks can capture the float associated with redeposited return items by processing a special float entry, which adjusts the customer's collected balance. It may be appropriate to use a simplified availability schedule to determine the correct amount of float to charge. For example, items in the bank's Federal Reserve district might be assigned one day of float, while all other items receive two days.

Float Reporting   8

Float reporting is the most visible tool of float management. A good float report is one of the best ways to focus management's attention on the float program. A good float report is the best way to advertise success. A mediocre float report gathers dust, while management turns its attention and support to other matters.

The purpose of float reporting is to inform bank management about the progress in float management. The reason for informing management about float is to establish and maintain the credibility of the float program, and thereby obtain the support needed for effective float management. Clear, concise, informative, and believable float reporting is a sign of strong float management. The discipline imposed by unambiguous float reporting helps to focus float management efforts and ensures accountability for float program results.

Regular float reporting also helps uncover trends that might go unnoticed if important data remained buried under mountains of standard financial reports. In preparing the monthly float report, a float manager is forced to distill the bottom-line meaning from the reams of statistics gathered in day-to-day float management. Once the important data are distilled, the float manager will understand where progress has been made and where opportunities exist.

The Float Report

A float report is a periodic summary of key float statistics and indicators of float management performance presented to bank management. The most common reporting frequency is monthly. A float report typically includes information for the current reporting period, as well as previous period statistics for comparison and analysis of trends.

Some basic statistics found on most float reports include: Aggregate Float, Aggregate Demand Deposits, Net Usable Funds (Demand Deposits minus Float), Float as a Percentage of Demand Deposits, the Clearing Ratio (average days to collect), and Length of Stay. Most include the same measures for the previous month; some track statistics for the year earlier period.

This type of report is adequate for answering such questions as, "How much float is there?" or "How long does it take to clear a check?" It does not, however, explain the significance of float in the bank. Management's concerns about float can be summed up in two questions:

- How much float should our bank have?

- How good is the bank's float management performance?

The typical float report does not answer these questions. This is because most float managers see float reporting as either a compulsory recording of float related data, or as a way of touting impressive float management successes. The former is almost never informative, while the latter is almost never credible. Instead, float managers should look at float reporting from the viewpoint of bank management, for whom reporting is intended. What management needs is an understandable and unambiguous assessment of the impact of float and float management on the bank as a whole.

One of the shortcomings of traditional float reporting is that it is not very good at explaining why float levels and other float-related statistics change. For example, an increase in aggregate float could be an indication of problems in float management, or it could just mean the bank is growing. An increase in the clearing ratio, indicating a longer average time to collect checks, could be the result of missed transit deadlines, or it could mean customers are depositing fewer local checks.

Float levels and performance measures can change for any of a number of reasons, and only a few of these are under the control of the bank or the float manager. What is needed is a way of analyzing the underlying reasons for float variances. Otherwise, the float manager will have a hard time maintaining credibility with bank management when the float report shows unexpected and unexplainable changes in float.

Volume, Mix, and Rate

Manufacturers analyze variances in budgeted product costs as a function of volume, mix, and rate. By segregating these factors, managers can determine whether changes in average or total product costs are due to internal factors, such as manufacturing efficiency and cost control, or to external factors, such as sales volume and product mix.

For a shoe manufacturer, volume would be the number of shoes produced, mix would be the relative volumes of each type of shoe produced, and rate would be the cost of producing each type of shoe. A typical budget variance analysis for the cost of producing shoes might look like Table 8.1.

Table 8.1

ABC SHOE MANUFACTURING
Cost of Goods Sold Analysis
Prior Period or Budget

Shoe Type	Volume		Unit Cost	Total COGS
Wingtip	100	11%	$11.50	$1,150
Loafer	200	22%	7.25	1,450
Sandal	600	67%	5.10	3,060
Total	900	100%	$6.29	$5,660

Current Period or Actual

Shoe Type	Volume		Unit Cost	Total COGS
Wingtip	180	20%	$11.50	$2,070
Loafer	200	23%	7.00	1,400
Sandal	500	57%	5.10	2,550
Total	880	100%	$6.84	$6,020

Table 8.1 *continued*

Reasons for Variance

Change in Volume - 20 fewer units X $6.29 average unit cost

($126)

Change in Mix - Higher percentage of wingtips and loafers   536

Change in Rate - Decrease of $0.25 per loafer X 200   (50)

Total Variance $360

In this case, total Cost of Goods Sold increased $360, even though total volume—the number of shoes produced—declined by 20 units. By itself, this would imply poor cost control, reflecting badly on the production manager. But all of the increased cost was attributable to a change in mix to a higher percentage of more costly shoes (wingtips and loafers). In fact, although the average cost per unit was up, the cost of wingtips and sandals was unchanged, and the cost of loafers actually declined.

Increased cost or reduced volume in a period will raise concerns with management. Through the use of volume, mix, and rate analysis, the production manager can address management concerns, thus separating the production manager's performance (reduction in the cost of producing loafers) from other external and uncontrollable factors.

Analyzing Changes in Float

The volume, mix, and rate approach to variance analysis can be applied to float reporting. The relevant factors are as follows:

• Volume—the total dollar value of transit items.

• Mix—the relative dollar volumes of checks classified as same-day, one-day, and two-day items. Categories are based on the availability typically associated with items bearing the same routing number, not the availability actually received. For example, if checks with a particular routing number generally are cleared in one day, all items with that routing number are categorized as one-day items, even if some take two days to clear. Without this type of categorization, one cannot accurately separate mix from rate.

- Rate—the clearing ratio, or average days to collect, for each class of items.

Table 8.2 illustrates volume, mix, and rate analysis of a change in float.

Table 8.2   ABC BANK Float Analysis (In Business Days)

Current Month

Float Category	Transit Volume ($ millions)		Days to Collect	Total Float ($ millions)
0 Day	50	5%	0.20	10
1 Day	750	75%	1.10	825
2 Day	200	20%	2.05	410
Total	1,000	100%	1.25	1,245

Previous Month

Float Category	Transit Volume ($ millions)		Days to Collect	Total Float ($ millions)
0 Day	100	11.1%	0.25	25
1 Day	600	66.7%	1.10	660
2 Day	200	22.2%	2.05	410
Total	900	100%	1.22	1,095

In this example, total float increased by $150 million, and the average time to collect lengthened by 0.03 days. But this was not because of poor float performance. Instead, the increase in days to collect was due to a change in mix that included fewer same-day items. Collection performance for same-day items actually improved, while one-day and two-day rates remained constant. The increase in float was due to the change in mix and an increase in volume, as shown in Table 8.3.

Table 8.3   Reasons for Variance

Change in Volume $100 million increase x 1.22 Days to Collect	$122 million
Change in Mix Shift of volume from 0-day to 1-day	31 million
Change in Rate Decrease of 0.05 Days to Collect for 0-day items	(3) million
Total Variance	$150 million

The increase in float attributable to an increase in volume is calculated by multiplying the total increase in transit volume by the average days to collect in the base period. This shows what the float increase would have been if only the transit volume, and not mix or rate, had increased (See Table. 8.4).

Table 8.4   The increase attributable to change in mix

Float Category	Current % of total	Previous % of total	Change	Current Volume	Previous Rate	Change in Float
0 Day	5%	− 11.1% =	(6.1%) x	1,000	x 0.25 days	=(15.3)
1 Day	75%	− 66.7% =	8.3% x	1,000	x 1.1 days	= 91.3
2 days	20%	− 20.2% =	2.2% x	1,000	x 2.05 days	=(45.1)
					Total	30.9

Although overall days to collect increased, this was due to the change in mix. Collection times for 1-day and 2-day items remained the same, while same-day items were collected an average of 0.05 days faster. So change in rate resulted in a net float reduction. The impact of a change in collection speed on float is calculated by multiplying the difference in collection times by current month volume for each float category.

Note that the example used business days instead of calendar days for the calculation of float variance. This was done to minimize variance due to weekends and holidays. When analyzed on a calendar day basis, the impact of changes in mix is more pronounced.

The technique of analyzing volume, mix, and rate is a way of determining how much of a change in float can be attributed to float management, and how much is due to other factors. Float management has little, if any, control over the volume and mix of deposits, but it should be held accountable for changes in collection time.

Performance Measures

In addition to explaining changes in aggregate float levels, float reporting should also provide relevant measures of float management performance in the following areas:

- Float Allocation.

- Holdover.

- Lost Availability.

- Cash Letter Fails.

Float Allocation

There are two key measures of float allocation: average negative/unallocated float and the percentage of float allocated to customers. Negative float occurs when a bank allocates more float to customer's accounts than it incurs on customer deposits. Unallocated float is float the bank incurs on customer deposits in excess of the amount it allocates to customers. Negative float is therefore the opposite of unallocated float. The average level of negative float is an indication of the overall value of float allocation, but it can be distorted by changes in volume. The percentage of float allocated is a better measurement of relative float management performance.

Banks often calculate two float allocation ratios. One is the percentage of deposit float incurred by the bank that is allocated to depositing customers. The other is the percentage of total bank float allocated, including float from such nondeposit sources as loan payments. Table 8.5 illustrates float allocation measurement.

**Table 8.5   ABC Bank Float Allocation Measurement
(In Millions)**

Float, by source:	
Customer deposits	$250
Loan payments	40
Other	10
Total Float	$300
Float allocated to customers	$285
Negative float — ($285 – 250)	$35
Float allocation:	
Deposit float — ($285/250) x 100	114 %
Bank float — ($285/$300 x 100	95 %

In this example, the bank has $35 million in negative float, meaning it allocated $35 million more float to customer accounts than it incurred on those accounts. This represents a 114 percent allocation of deposit float. However, allocated float was less than total bank float, resulting in bank float allocation of 95 percent.

Holdover and Lost Availability

Holdover represents transit checks received in a day's work but not processed in time to meet that day's cash letter dispatch deadlines, resulting in an increase in float for the bank. Important measures of holdover are average holdover and holdover as a percentage of total cash letter sends.

Lost availability represents transit checks not processed in time to obtain the best availability of the day. For example, if checks drawn on a particular endpoint must be dispatched by 9:00 P.M. to receive one-day availability, items for that endpoint sent in later cash letters and receiving two-day float represent lost availability. Average lost availability and lost availability as a percentage of total cash letter sends are the most commonly reported measures, although some banks report the percentage of transit dollar volume receiving best availability instead.

Table 8.6 illustrates the measures of holdover and lost availability:

Table 8.6   ABC BANK Holdover and Lost Availability (In Millions)

Cash Letter Sends (Fed & Correspondents)	$1,000
Holdover	$ 2
Holdover %	0.2 %
Lost Availability	$ 55
Lost Availability %	5.5 %
Best Availability %	94.5 %

Note that both holdover and lost availability measures are calculated on the basis of cash letter sends to the Federal Reserve and correspondent banks instead of total transit volume. This is because clearing house exchange volume, the other major component of transit volume, is usually subject to an early, obtainable next-day deadline. Including clearing house volume would skew holdover and lost availability measures.

Cash Letter Fails

Cash letter fails represent cash letters dispatched by the bank that do not arrive at the correspondent bank or Federal Reserve check processing site before its deadline, and therefore suffer a loss in availability. Transportation delays and mis-routed packages are typical reasons for cash letter fails.

Banks usually report the aggregate dollar value of cash letter fails. Another measure is cash letter fails as a percentage of cash letter sends.

How Much Float?

Analysis of volume, mix, and rate, combined with measures of float allocation, holdover, and lost availability, provides answers to the question: "How good is the bank's float management performance?" But something else is needed to answer the other question posed by bank management: "How much float should the bank have?"

In most cases, the answer will not be an absolute amount. Because float is a by-product of deposit taking, float will fluctuate with deposits. Furthermore, the mix of items deposited can have a substantial impact on float levels, making them even more volatile.

Instead, many banks have found it better to create dynamic float targets that respond to deposit activity. One such measure is based on check-processing throughput. Throughput in check processing is measured as the percentage of checks in each availability category (ie., one-day, two-day) that are processed in time to receive best availability. For example, a bank might establish the following throughput goals:

0-Day	85 percent receive same-day availability
1-Day	90 percent receive one-day availability
2-Day	95 percent receive two-day availability

Based on these goals, a bank's total float target for a period could be calculated as shown in Table 8.7.

Table 8.7   ABC BANK Float Target (In Millions)

Float Category	Transit Volume	Throughput Goal	0-Day Goal	1-Day Goal	2-Day Goal	3-Day Goal	Float Target
0-Day	50	85 %	42.5	7.5			7.5
1-Day	750	90 %		675.0	75		825.0
2-Day	200	95 %			190	10	410.0
Total	1,000		42.5	682.5	265	10	1,242.5

The float target was calculated by first dividing the volume for each float category according to availability goals. For example, if the throughput goal for 0-day items is 85 percent, the availability goal is 85 percent 0-day, 15 percent one-day. The amount under each availability goal was then multiplied by the number of days availability to determine the float target.

Float targets are designed to provide a benchmark for evaluating float levels that adjust to changes in volume and mix. Because float targets are based on item processing throughput goals, they also serve as a way of measuring workflow management performance. Factors such as system downtime, reject rates, staffing levels (including allowance for vacation and sickness), proof productivity, and inbound transportation should be managed to maintain acceptable float levels. Throughput goals link workflow to target float levels, making item processing performance an integral and measurable component of float management.

Throughput goals should be reviewed periodically and adjusted to reflect changes in the check processing environment. Permanent changes in work receipt patterns, transportation schedules, and machine capacity are a few of the factors that would warrant modification of throughput standards, resulting in adjusted float targets.

Improved Float Reporting

Armed with techniques for float variance analysis, key performance measures, and throughput based float standards, the float manager is able to create a more informative float report that targets the concerns of bank management. No single "standard" float report is appropriate for every bank; each bank should develop float reporting tailored to the needs and concerns of its own management. The following general principals, however, usually apply at most institutions.

First, be sure that float reporting is consistent with financial reporting. At most banks, this means that average float levels, clearing ratios, and other items should be reported on the basis of calendar days, not business days. Although business days are usually best for everyday analysis and tracking, bank-wide financial reporting is usually done on a calendar-day basis. If the float report does not reconcile to financial reports because of a calendar-day/business-day difference, senior management will question the accuracy of the float report.

Calendar-day reporting tends to amplify the effect of changes in mix. It can also skew collection times. Distortions in float levels caused by differences in weekends and holidays can be explained as part of a separate variance analysis, as shown in Table 8.8.

Table 8.8   Reasons for Variance
Adjusted for Calendar versus Business Days

Change in Volume	
$100 million increase X 1.22 Days to Collect	$122 million
Change in Mix	
Shift of volume from 0-day to 1-day	31 million
Change in Rate	
Decrease of 0.05 Days to Collect for 0-day items	(3) million
Calendar vs. Business Days	
Two more holidays/weekend days	10 million
Total Variance	$160 million

Another guideline for float reporting is that management wants answers, not explanations. The float report should present important float information, not the detailed calculations used to produce it. The spreadsheets used to analyze float variances might be of great interest to you, but should probably not be included in the float report. Too much detail tends to bury important information.

Use charts to illustrate important trends and relationships, such as changes in float levels, deposit mix, and performance against goals. Float management must vie with dozens of other areas for the time and attention of bank management, so the float report should provide essential information in a format that is easy to understand at a glance. Graphics are one of the best ways of packaging information for busy executives. A first page summary is another way of condensing essential float information. The summary can present the most important float indicators, providing an overview of bank float. Subsequent pages can go into greater detail or show long-term trends.

Table 8.9 is an example of a float report that illustrates the techniques presented in this chapter.

Table 8.9   FLOAT REPORT

Float National Bank January 1991
(Amounts in millions)

	January 91	*December 90*	
Average Daily Float	$1,245.0	$1,095.0	+ 13.7 %
Float Target	$1,242.5	$1,104.3	
Variance From Target	2.5	(9.3)	
Float Allocation			
Total Bank	101.2 %	102.3 %	
Depository Products	114.4 %	112.8 %	
Negative Float	$179.4	$140.1	
Transit Volume	$1,000.0	$900.0	+ 11.1 %
Clearing Ratio (Days to Collect)	1.245 days	1.216 days	+ 0.029 days
Length of Stay	2.13 days	2.18 days	- 0.05 days

Reasons for Increase in Float

Change in Volume $100 million increase X 1.22 Days to Collect	$122 million
Change in Mix Shift of volume from 0-day to 1-day	31 million
Change in Rate Decrease of 0.05 Days to Collect for 0-day items	(3) million
Total Increase	$150 million

Float: A Depository Product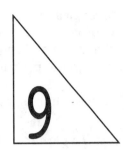

In chapter 4, we discussed the relationship of float to product management. By allocating float to depository products, it becomes an explicit cost component of those products, and therefore influences product managers' pricing activities. In addition, by associating revenues with negative float, the product manager is given a way to fine tune customer availability to maximize income.

Many banks have gone even further by managing float itself as a product. Float has many of the same characteristics as other bank products. Float has value, in much the same way that loaned funds have value. Like loans, the value of float is a function of time and interest rates. Float can be priced and charged against account analysis. Float pricing is also a factor in competition for customers, especially in cash management and correspondent banking.

Decisions about float allocation and pricing can have a major impact on the earnings and competitive position of the bank. Applying the techniques of product management to float is one way of ensuring the impact is positive.

Product Management

Product management originated in the consumer packaged goods industry in the 1930s, and it has since spread to most U.S. business sectors. Banking was relatively late in adopting product management, but in the 1980s most major banks embraced the idea in at least some fashion. Product management is most prevalent in cash management and mass market retail areas such as credit cards and deposit accounts.

Unlike the packaged goods industries, where product managers typically have a great deal of autonomy and authority, bank product managers usually serve in more of an analytical and advisory role. Most pricing decisions must be approved by a pricing committee of senior managers, while the heads of various business units retain authority for marketing and product support.

At most banks, the product manager's role is three-fold:

1. To gather and analyze product information.

2. To make recommendations for product pricing, structure, support and marketing.

3. To coordinate the efforts of other bank departments involved in developing, producing, marketing, delivering, and supporting the product.

Product managers also play a central role in new product development, usually as project managers and coordinators.

Managing Float as a Product

Before a bank can begin managing float as a product, it must be committed to treating the assignment of availability to deposits as a pricing function, not simply a passing through of float. Traditionally, banks' rationale for allocating float to accounts was cost recovery; the goal was to break even. But if float is treated as a product, the availability schedule is the price list, and negative float is the profit margin.

There are a number of ways that banks can apply the concept of product management to float. One, of course, is to create the position of a float product manager. The other is to have the float manager assume the role of a product manager for float. Or a bank can group several float sensitive products, such as correspondent check clearing and corporate checking, under a single manager with float management responsibilities.

Regardless of the organizational structure, the float product manager is charged with maximizing the profitability of the float product, primarily through the creation of negative float and float pricing. The main tools used in float product management are availability schedules, account analysis, and depository product structure.

Availability Schedules

One area where float product managers sometimes have a greater influence than managers of more traditional products is pricing. This is because the primary element in float pricing is the assignment of availability, but availability schedules are often outside a bank's formal pricing structure. So while changing the pricing of a checking account might require the approval of a senior management pricing committee, changes in availability can often be made with a minimum of red tape.

Most availability decisions arise when the bank begins clearing a particular class of checks faster. The issue is whether to pass the improved availability on to the customer or to retain the gain as negative float. Under the product management concept, this is a pricing issue, and the decision should be made according to product pricing criteria.

Products are priced according to demand, cost, and competition. For float, the product cost is the float incurred by the bank. Competition is exemplified by the availability schedules of other banks. Demand is harder to judge, but it can best be described as sensitivity to availability. Some customers, especially those depositing large-dollar checks, are quite sensitive to availability, while others are less so.

Availability schedules should balance these factors to maximize float earnings. The availability schedule should at least cover bank costs by recovering bank float. The availability schedules for competing banks should be monitored to determine the "market price" for each endpoint. And availability should reflect an understanding of the customer's sensitivity to float.

Account Analysis

If float is priced through availability schedules, then **account analysis** is how float charges are billed. The effectiveness of account analysis in turning negative float into revenue is a crucial element in float product management.

The main way account analysis turns negative float into revenue is by causing corporate customers to hold greater account balances than they would have otherwise. This is effective with three types of customers. One type is the cash management conscious customer who actively manages accounts to avoid excess balances. Another type is the customer who maintains minimal collected balances and pays fees instead of compensating balances. The third type is the customer who deliberately holds a predetermined level of excess balances and manages the account to that balance. All three types will increase account balances to cover uncollected funds.

The float product manager should know the composition of the account base in order to understand the effectiveness of float pricing. Float pricing efforts should be directed at those customer segments most responsive to changes in uncollected funds.

The float manager should also understand how float is allocated to deposits, and how allocated float is passed on to the account analysis system. Of particular concern are any gaps in the process that can result in lost float assignments. Common culprits are such items as rejected credits, which may not be assigned correct float when re-entered, and error adjustments, which often are posted as floatless entries, even though they are substitutes for float bearing deposits. The float product manager should also ensure that any float adjustments made to the account analysis are reflected in the compensating balance calculation, and not just in historical data.

Some banks have another way of charging for float on account analysis. Each day a customer carries a negative collected balance, the bank charges a fee equal to the customer's normal loan rate, instead of merely reducing the average collected balance for the month. The rationale is that the bank is giving the customer use of the uncollected funds through a sort of informal loan.

Depository Product Structure

As discussed in chapter 2, banks can obtain substantial benefits through such practices as late evening clearing house exchange or earlier ledger deadlines. Often, however, this may require restructuring of depository products. For example, cash letter customers may be required to separate on-us items from transit items to allow same-day credit for the on-us checks. Deferred posting of cash concentration entries may require changes in balance reporting.

Market Segmentation

One of the key concepts of product management is market segmentation. Since different segments have different demands, products are tailored accordingly. In float product management, this is accomplished by offering multiple availability schedules. Each is tailored to the float sensitivity of a particular market segment.

For example, the most float sensitive customers are often securities brokers, who typically deposit a low volume of large-dollar value checks. Brokers want the absolute best availability; they do not want to lose a day of interest on the occasional multi-million dollar check. If a bank had only one availability schedule, and based availability on the demands of its brokerage customers, there would be little opportunity to create negative float, because improvements in check collections would be passed on to all customers immediately.

Retailers, however, are more concerned with item pricing than availability. Retailers tend to deposit a high volume of small checks, most of which are local. For most retailers, losing a day of availability on a $40 check is better than paying higher fees.

If a bank wanted to be competitive in attracting both securities brokers and retail stores with a single availability and pricing schedule, it would have to offer premium availability at a bargain basement item price. The lower deposited check fees would be wasted on the brokers, while the better availability would be of little interest to the retailers.

Market segmentation allows the bank to compete for both groups without giving up income needlessly. By offering different availability schedules to different segments, the bank can tailor products to the unique demands of each. Item pricing would be adjusted accordingly, so that negative float lost in giving premium availability is at least partially recouped through higher fees. Sometimes, markets can be segmented within a single product. For example, cash letter availability schedules sometimes offer later deadlines or premium availability for checks that are sorted separately, usually at a higher price.

Of course, the ability to segment markets through multiple availability schedules is subject to limits. Some systems cannot support multiple float tables for availability assignment, and most are limited to a finite number of schedules. In addition, the segmentation should not be so complex that it cannot be understood by the bank's account officers and by customers.

Float product managers should remember two important points in developing market segmentation strategies. One is that most banks can only serve a limited number of market segments profitably. The other is that segmentation should be coordinated with other products to ensure a unified effort. Most customer segments require a range of products, so the float product manager should target those segments that are part of the bank's overall business strategy.

"Over-recovery" and Nondeposit Float

Float is a depository product, but banks incur float in performing a number of nondeposit functions. One of the important issues in float product management is whether the negative float generated by depository products should cover bank float from nondepository sources.

The issue of recovering all bank float through depository products is not strictly within the scope of float product management. But if a bank has established a goal of full bank float recovery, the only effective way to achieve this is through aggressive float pricing, which is a product management function. Most of the float will be recovered through depository products.

One alternative is to price nondeposit float. The cost of float associated with trust services, for example, can be included in fees for trust management and transaction charges. Some banks assess an explicit float charge for bond coupon collections handled for immediate credit. Such charges, however, usually fall short of the level needed to recover the float associated with nondepository services.

The Future of Float

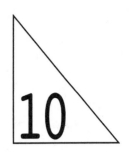

Float in the United States is largely a product of its check collection system. Because checks must be delivered physically to the paying bank, float is inherent in check collections. The limits of transportation and geography make it impossible to wring float out of the current system. The large number of paying institutions compounds the difficulty.

Check writing, and therefore float, is a phenomenon primarily associated with English speaking countries, and Americans are the world's most prolific check writers. U.S. check volumes now surpass 50 billion items a year, far more than the rest of the world combined, making checks the dominant form of non-cash payment. Because of the predominance of checks, large-scale float is almost uniquely American. Most other countries rely on either cash or various credit transfer systems for the bulk of their payment activity, avoiding float almost entirely.

Payments in Other Countries

In many ways, the future of float is the future of checks. This chapter looks at some of the proposals for changing U.S. payment systems, and the impact they would have on float. But first, let us see how the American check collection system compares with payment systems in other countries.

Giro Systems

The predominant noncash payment system in Continental Europe and Japan is the giro. Unlike checks, which are debit drafts that must be collected from the paying bank, giro payments are credit transfers. Someone wishing to pay by giro initiates the payment at their own bank, which transfers the money to the recipient's bank. Because it is a credit transfer, there is no risk of paying against insufficient funds, and the paying customer's account is debited immediately, eliminating float.

Giro payments are used most frequently for bill payments and payrolls. The party making payment need only know the recipient's bank and account number. Companies usually include this information on their bills, and employers keep employee account numbers on payroll records. Individuals initiate payment by filling out a standard form that is either presented or mailed to their bank, while corporations usually initiate payment electronically or by tape. Customers without giro accounts can usually pay bills or receive payroll giro transfers in cash at any bank branch or post office.

The earliest giros systems were established by post offices in Europe. In many countries, the postal savings bank is a popular retail depository institution. Giros were developed as a way of providing an alternative to cash for low-value payments. A customer could go into any post office and make a giro payment, paying the teller cash or transferring funds from a postal savings account. The giro system made it unnecessary to send cash through the mail.

Postal giros became so popular that the banks in most countries developed their own giro systems to remain competitive. The bank and postal giro systems typically operate side-by-side, and there is usually a link between the two allowing interchange of payments.

Giros were initially paper-based systems, but most are converting to electronic clearing. One advantage of giros is that conversion to EFT is virtually transparent to the user. Individuals can still initiate payments as they did before, but the bank can truncate the items upon receipt, converting them to electronic transactions. This process is made easier because giro entries are standard documents.

The Canadian Check Collection System

In 1980, Canadian banks automated check collections through the Canadian Payments Association (CPA). The Canadian system allows one-day collection of checks drawn anywhere in Canada, despite the remoteness of many communities in the vast, sparsely populated western provinces.

The CPA even claims to have eliminated the cost of float through its practice of backdated settlement.

CPA membership is mandatory for all Canadian banks. The largest are direct clearers, with accounts at the Bank of Canada for settlement. The others are indirect clearers, which must settle through correspondent accounts at direct clearers.

Early on the day following deposit, Canadian banks exchange checks or magnetic tapes at ten regional clearing centers. The clearing banks calculate a net settlement for each center by 11:00 A.M. Settlement occurs at the Bank of Canada, by 3:00 P.M. The settling entries are backdated, so the depository bank receives credit on the date of deposit. Banks therefore give customers same-day credit for deposited checks.

Under the Canadian system, the checks are delivered to paying banks or, in the case of smaller institutions, their clearing banks. But physical delivery of the items is a separate function from settlement, so the limitations of transportation do not delay the flow of funds.

The Canadian check collection system is considered by many the most efficient paper-based payment system in the world. A number of factors contribute to the success of the program:

- The ten regional centers eliminate the need to transport checks across country before settlement.

- Canadian banking is dominated by six large banks, which operate nationwide. These banks act as direct clearers and can accept checks at any of the ten regional centers, simplifying settlement.

- The limited number and large size of direct clearers has resulted in economies of scale, justifying a high degree of automation and facilitating coordination of operations and uniform procedures.

- The establishment of the CPA was mandated by law, and membership is compulsory. Highly competitive banks and often distrustful smaller institutions have been compelled to cooperate in developing a system that works well for all members.

Although the Canadian check collection system seems to have eliminated float by backdating settlement, this is not a complete solution. Banks are not able to withdraw or replenish balances until settlement, so the backdated entry is only of use in calculating the bank's reserve position. The ability to invest funds depends more on future balance management activity, which can take advantage of the value of backdated entries. For most institutions, net settlement entries are relatively small in comparison with reserve account balances because the value of items presented is roughly the same as the value of receipts, so the distortions of backdating are manageable.

U.S. Proposals

Since the development of the Automated Clearing House network in the 1970s, there have been many proposals to use electronic clearings to either replace or to improve the current check collection system. Some proposals were studied then abandoned, while others progressed to pilot projects. A few are working on an operational basis. The following summaries describe some of the ideas for a more efficient check collection system.

Interbank Truncation

The main impediment to improved check clearing is the burden of transporting checks to the paying bank for presentment. If the depository bank or a clearing bank could hold the item and substitute an electronic payment, a process known as truncation, it could avoid the transportation costs and delays involved inherent in physical presentment.

The disadvantages of truncation are that the paying bank does not have the opportunity to examine the check to verify the drawer's signature, and the item is not available for subsequent research. Checks cannot be returned in the customer's statement, and providing copies of checks requires contacting the truncating bank.

Under the auspices of the National Association for Check Safekeeping (NACS), a number of major banks and the Federal Reserve operate an interbank check truncation program for corporate checks. Participating banks intercept eligible checks, substituting an ACH transaction.

The program has established strict guidelines for the types of checks eligible for truncation. Most are dividend checks and similar corporate items. Customers must agree to truncation. Checks eligible for truncation are designated by a "2" in a reserved location on the MICR line, and participating banks agree to assist each other in researching items truncated for other banks. Due to the eligibility requirements, the volume of checks truncated under the NACS is negligible in comparison to overall check volumes. But the NACS scheme has shown that under the right circumstances, check truncation is feasible.

The Federal Reserve System offers check truncation to financial institutions, stopping checks at the Federal Reserve Bank before presentation. The largest use of the Federal Reserve service is for official checks issued by credit unions. In 1990, the National Automated Clearing House Association (NACHA), NACS and the Federal Reserve initiated a pilot to truncate high volumes of low-dollar value checks written for consumer products rebates. The checks, written on a Minnesota bank, bear a "3" in the truncation field of the MICR line.

Electronic Check Clearing

In 1981, and again in 1988, the Federal Reserve System studied the feasibility of developing a nationwide electronic check clearing system. The idea was to develop a system that would accommodate truncation of eligible items, but that would also allow broad based electronic clearing of other checks.

At the time, both studies concluded that full-scale electronic clearing would not be feasible. Truncation of all items, or low dollar items, was deemed unfeasible because of the need to provide for signature verification, as well as for a belief that many consumers would demand to continue receiving paid checks with their statements. A system that employed electronic presentment and settlement, with later physical delivery of checks, was deemed to be too complicated, while promising little reduction in overall costs and only marginal float reduction. One stumbling block was the need to accommodate thousands of small institutions that would be unable to afford the technology required for electronic clearings.

The 1988 study suggested that electronic check clearing might be a viable option in remote areas such as the Upper Peninsula of Michigan. It also saw much potential in existing truncation programs. The study held out the hope of wide-scale electronic presentment of check images instead of the items themselves, although such a system would require substantial advances in image technology, telecommunications, and standards.

In the late 1980s, banks in the Houston Clearing House began exchanging magnetic tapes in advance of physical presentment, a practice soon adopted by other clearing houses. And in 1990, a number of banks formed the Electronic Check Clearing House Association (ECCHO) to begin limited national electronic exchange and clearings. Under the ECCHO program, participating banks exchange electronic information at night and deliver the checks the following day. Electronic exchange allows banks to begin processing as much as one day earlier.

ACH Conversion

Despite the success of some promising pilot programs, check truncation and electronic check clearing have had negligible impact on the check collection system as a whole. The overwhelming majority of checks are simply not eligible for truncation under existing schemes, and electronic exchange is still limited to banks that have already established direct links for physical presentment.

The most promising alternative to current truncation programs or electronic exchange would be the conversion of checks to ACH payments. The advantages are that the ACH system is already in place and works well, and virtually all financial institutions can accept ACH payments. Conversion is also well within the capabilities of existing technology. But in order to allow movement to ACH check conversion, the U.S. banking system must overcome a number of obstacles.

Laws and ACH rules would need to be changed to allow conversion of paper items to electronic payments without the explicit consent of the paying bank. Conversion is now allowed only when both the paying bank and the truncating bank agree, within the context of a truncation program. The capacity of the ACH system would also need to be increased substantially to accommodate the volume of converted checks if the idea becomes popular. Check volume is currently 40 times ACH volume.

Converting banks would need to develop cost effective ways of including the payee in the ACH payment. This information is not on the MICR line. Instead of manually encoding or keying this information, the depository bank could determine the payee by identifying the deposit account, although care must be taken to exclude third-party checks.

Customers would need to accept a descriptive statement instead of return of paid checks. There is, however, a precedent for this. In the 1970s, both Visa and MasterCard switched to descriptive statements with little customer resistance.

Signature verification responsibility would need to be eliminated or altered. Fraudulent or unauthorized checks would not be discovered until after the customer received a statement listing the transaction, so reversal could take months. Liability could be shifted to the depositing customer, who is likely to have a relationship with the check writer, and would therefore be in a position to verify the authenticity of the checks. Banks would therefore need to have a good, ongoing relationship with depositing customers to ensure that they would honor chargebacks, in much the same way that banks clearing credit card drafts monitor their merchant customers. This would make ACH conversion most feasible for commercial deposits. Most checks, however, originate in commercial deposits.

Procedures would need to be developed for return of electronically collected items. Customers who deposit paper items are unlikely to be satisfied with an ACH return notice. The converting bank would probably be required to outsort return items upon notification. To avoid extensive resorting, strict schedules would need to be developed for returns, with penalties for late returns.

None of these obstacles is insurmountable. I believe the benefits of ACH conversion—reduction of float, faster handling of returns, and reduction of transportation costs—far outweigh the difficulties and expense of implementation.

Intra-day Float

Even if the check collection system is reformed, new types of float are emerging that call for innovative approaches to float management. One of the more unusual concepts is intra-day float. Today, bank float is created when an item is deposited one day but payment is received the following day or later. Because bank accounting and interest calculations are based on business days, same-day collections do not create float, regardless of what time of day transactions are posted.

In the interest of controlling risk, however, the Federal Reserve has established guidelines restricting "daylight overdrafts." Daylight overdrafts occur when a bank makes payments out of its reserve account or a correspondent account in excess of account balances, covering the deficit later in the day. At the end of the day after all transactions are posted, the account has a positive balance, but for a period during the day, it was overdrawn. Corporate accounts at banks are also subject to daylight overdrafts.

Under one proposal, the Federal Reserve would begin to charge interest on daylight overdrafts to discourage the practice. By doing so, the Fed would be associating an explicit cost with delayed receipt of same day payment. The gap between the sending of an outgoing payment and the receipt of funds to cover would be intra-day float. Banks might begin trading same-day funds and assessing intra-day float charges against corporate customers' accounts.

Another development that could spur the development of intra-day float concepts is the growing internationalization of banking. Major banks now trade in money markets around the globe, and some have opened 24-hour trading desks. To accommodate round-the-clock activity, some banks are moving to real-time accounting. Participation in global markets places a premium on early delivery of funds, allowing banks to take advantage of arbitrage opportunities in other countries.

William Swords' Ten Best Float Tips

1. Float is not bad. Excessive float is bad. A healthy, growing bank will experience growth in float. Remember: No bank ever failed from too much float; most banks fail because of a conspicuous lack of float.

2. Understanding float is not that hard. I know that I am breaking the sacred oath taken by all good float managers when I make this statement, but the age of enlightenment is long overdue.

3. It pays to advertise. Management needs to know when things are going well and when they are not. Don't inundate management with information, but keep them informed with a clear, concise, and constant flow of information. A little "razzle-dazzle" associated with float savings is never inappropriate.

4. In the check clearing business, never accept less than a two-to-one payback. Check clearing float can be reduced by seeking out clearing agents offering the best availability. While float will be reduced, transportation expense and bank clearing fees will usually increase. If the estimated benefits are not two times the estimated costs, I would look long and hard before I implemented the send. Remember that we need to overestimate benefits and underestimate costs.

5. Have someone else choose your interest rate. All float reduction efforts are approved by someone in management before implementation, and the float manager must prepare a cost/benefit analysis. Float benefits are normally determined by multiplying the additional available funds by the applicable interest rate at which the funds can be invested. No matter how large the benefit, no matter how simple the implementation, someone will inevitably ask, "Where did you get your rate? I think you used the wrong rate!" Of course, when asked, you can always answer "From Allen Greenspan."

6. Keep it simple. There are a lot of key indicators used by float managers to measure their performance and their bank's performance. Choose two or three to focus on and stick with them.

7. Price, not availability, sells deposit business. As the float manager, your job is to understand the relationship between price and availability. Unfortunately, most customers are not float managers. Most customers are ordinary people, and ordinary people understand price, not float. There are, however, some exceptions, but that is why you have multiple availability schedules.

8. The purpose of the availability schedule is to impress and confuse the user (not necessarily in that order). Fortunately, most availability schedules are prepared by marketing people, many uniquely suited for the task.

9. Be kind to the account officer who calls for your help. Remember: the account officer will only call when they have completely exhausted all known means of resolving the problem (When all else fails, read the instructions). In addition, the account officer will normally have a customer who feels ignored and misled. So take a deep breath and be kind.

10. If your spouse calls you up, and in a cooing voice suggests that you get together for a little woo-woo, hang up the phone and beat a path to your designated rendezvous. In the great scheme of things, float don't matter, loving do.

GLOSSARY

ACH: See Automated Clearing House.

Account Analysis: A periodic evaluation by a bank of the value of customer account balances as compensation for customer usage of bank products and services. Account analysis calculates an earnings credit for balances that is used to offset the value of priced services. The earnings credit is usually calculated on the basis of Collected Balances, Available Balances, or Investable Balances, making account analysis the primary means of realizing the benefits of allocating float to corporate customers.

Allocated Float: Bank Float identified and associated with a customer or internal department of the bank. Allocated Float is the sum of Customer Float and Internal Bank Float allocated to specific bank units or departments. Allocated Float is often expressed as a percentage of total Bank Float. If Allocated Float exceeds total Bank Float, float allocation is greater than 100 percent.

Automated Clearing House: An association of financial institutions that exchange electronic payments on a regular basis. The acronym ACH is commonly used for Automated Clearing House and to describe the type of payments made through an ACH. The National Automated Clearing House Association (NACHA), an association of Automated Clearing Houses, establishes the rules and formats for exchange of ACH payments.

Availability

Unencumbered access to deposited funds. Also used to describe the timing for the granting of Availability (e.g., if a bank grants Availability of funds on the second day after deposit for a certain class of checks, it is said to give two-day Availability).

Availability Schedule:

A table published by depositary banks or check clearing intermediary banks advertising or disclosing availability of check deposits. An availability schedule generally lists the float allocated to deposits according to the routing numbers of the checks deposited and the deposit deadline.

Available Balance:

A sum of money representing deposit account balances against which the bank has placed no restrictions on withdrawal or investment.

Balance Sheet Management

The practice of reducing the amount of float and related nonearning assets on a bank's general ledger, thereby reducing total assets and boosting capital ratios. The goal of balance sheet management is to decrease capital requirements and increase Return on Assets (ROA) and Return on Equity (ROE). Balance sheet management accomplishes float reduction by coordinating the processing of deposits and payments with more advantageous posting of accounting entries.

Bank Float:

A sum of money, recorded on the financial books of a bank, representing checks and other financial instruments that are outstanding and in the process of collection.

Book Balance: See Ledger Balance.

Booked Float: A sum of money, representing checks and other financial instruments, that is outstanding and in the process of collection, that has been recorded on the financial books of a bank, company, or individual.

Cash and Due From Accounts: A balance sheet category on a bank's general ledger comprising various asset accounts including, Vault Cash and Currency, Due From Bank Accounts, and Cash Items in the Process of Collection, as well as various work-in-process and suspense accounts. The Cash and Due From Accounts category is usually the largest nonearning financial asset category, and it is where most float on bank books resides.

Cash Item: A check or other financial instrument payable upon presentment to the paying bank, or a check or other financial instrument accepted for deposit by a Depositary Banks or a Check Clearing Intermediry Banks. A financial instrument that is cleared on behalf of a customer but that is not accepted for deposit is not a Cash Item to the depositor, although it may be presented as a Cash Item to the Paying Bank by the check clearing bank. The Federal Reserve requires that checks meet certain standards, such as MICR encoding of the routing number, in order to be accepted as cash items for its check clearing services.

Cash Letter: A package of cash items sent to a Check Clearing Intermediary bank for deposit and collection, including a listing of checks, a deposit ticket, and transmittal documents.

Check: A negotiable demand draft payable at a financial institution. Under Federal Reserve Regulation CC, checks, drafts, or warrants payable by the U.S. Treasury or state or local governments are considered checks, as well as other items such as certain money orders and travelers cheques.

**Check Clearing
Float:**   Collection float associated with checks.

**Check Clearing
Intermediary:**   A bank that clears checks for other banks. Also called a Clearing Agent.

Check Float: A sum of money representing checks that are outstanding and in the process of collection.

Check Kite   A type of fraud that takes advantage of check collection float to obtain the use of funds that appear to be on deposit but do not actually exist. Check Kiting schemes typically employ several checking accounts at different banks. The perpetrator deposits checks drawn on one account into another, on which checks are drawn to fund another, and so on, eventually funding the original account. By repeating this process, often with many variations to disguise the pattern, a skilled Check Kiter can parlay an insignificant initial account balance into large sums of fictitious money. In some instances, the funds are then withdrawn, leaving one or more banks with losses. Check Kiting may also be used to create balances that are in effect an unauthorized, interest-free loan, which is later repaid by the deposit of actual funds.

Clearing Agent: See Check Clearing Intermediary

Clearing House: An association of financial institutions that exchange checks or other financial instruments on a regular basis. The Clearing House association establishes rules for exchanging items, sets exchange deadlines, and provides for settlement among its members. Most Clearing Houses are local, including financial institutions within a single city or metropolitan area, or regional, covering part or all of a state.

Clearing House Float: Collection float associated with cash items cleared through a clearing house.

Collected Balance: A sum of money representing deposit account balances in excess of Customer Float allocated to the account. Ledger Balance minus Customer Float equals Collected Balance. The Collected Balance is the bank's approximation of monies on deposit for which the bank has received investable funds for deposited items.

Collection Float: Float representing checks and other financial instruments deposited in a bank for collection, for which the depositor has not received full availability of funds. Also called Deposit Float.

Correspondent Bank: A bank that provides services to another bank, or a bank that receives a service form another bank. The bank receiving the service is sometimes referred to as the respondent bank. Correspondent services include check clearing, loan participation, wholesale funds transfer, international transactions, and securities clearing.

Customer Float: Bank Float allocated to specific customers, reducing account balances available for withdrawal, investment or earnings credit against bank fees. Customer Float is allocated to the accounts of customers depositing items for collection. Customer Float allocated in excess actual Bank Float incurred on customer deposits is called Negative Float or Reverse Float. Customer Float is also referred to as Priced Float.

Deposit Float: See Collection Float.

Depositary Bank: The first financial institution to receive deposited items entering the banking system, sometimes referred to as the Bank of First Deposit.

Direct Presentment: Presentment of checks directly to the Paying Bank for collection. Contrasted with check collection through Clearing Agents.

Due From: Used to describe a bank's deposit accounts at other banks. Due From accounts carry balances that are "due from" the other bank on demand or on maturity. Checks and other items sent to other banks for collection are usually deposited into Due From accounts. International Due From accounts are often called Nostro accounts.

Due To: Used to describe deposits accounts held by other banks. Due To accounts carry balances that are "due to" another bank on demand or on maturity. Checks and other items received from other banks for collection are usually deposited into Due To accounts. International Due To accounts are often called Vostro accounts.

Encoding: The process of inscribing the dollar amount or other data in magnetic ink on checks and other items to prepare them for automated capture and sorting.

Endpoint: The financial institution at which a check is payable and to which it must be presented for collection. An endpoint is identified by its unique nine-digit Routing Number.

Federal Reserve Float: Funds the Federal Reserve System has credited to a bank's reserve account for checks deposited for collection, but for which the Federal Reserve has not received funds from the paying bank. The Federal Reserve System credits deposits on a deferred basis, according to its published availability schedule, so Federal Reserve Float represents checks not cleared within that schedule. This is in contrast to commercial bank practice, which is to credit deposits immediately, but allocate float to the depositor's account. Therefore, Federal Reserve Float is analogous to Positive Float at a commercial bank. Federal Reserve Float is often referred to as Fed Float.

Float:

A sum of money representing checks and other financial instruments that are outstanding and in the process of collection.

Holdover:

Transit checks received in one day's work but not processed in time to meet that day's cash letter deadlines, resulting in an increase in float for the bank.

Internal Bank Float:

Float a bank incurs in its role as a check issuer or a check recipient.

Investable Balance:

A sum of money representing deposit account balances available for external investment, or on which the customer may earn interest or credit against bank fees (if applicable).

Ledger Balance:

A sum of money representing the bank's record of deposit account balances after the positng of all debits and credits, before deducting Uncollected Funds. The Ledger Balance is the account balance reported for accounting purposes. Ledger Balance equals Collected Balance plus Uncollected Funds. The Ledger Balance is also referred to as the Book Balance.

Ledger Deadline: The latest time at which a bank will accept deposits or cash letters for same-day credit toward Ledger Balance. Also known as Deposit Cutoff, Ledger Cutoff, Deposit Deadline, and Cash Letter Cutoff.

Lockbox: A remittance processing service service provided by banks to corporate customers to reduce Mail Float, Processing Float, and Collection Float. Lockbox services reduce mail float by using unique ZIP codes and post office boxes, with frequent mail pick-up from the post office throughout the early morning. Processing float is minimized by the use of a streamlined, multi-shift processing environment. Lockboxes are generally designed to process the check for immediate deposit, replacing it with a photocopy that is returned with accompanying remittance documents to the company for posting to accounts receivable records. Check collection float is reduced because the check is deposited early in the processing day, and it is therefore able to meet earlier deadlines for check clearing and presentment.

Magnetic Ink Character Recognition: A technology that allows the automated reading of information by imprinting specially formed characters on an item in a metalicized ink that responds to a magnetic field in the reading equipment.

Mail Float: A component of the float cycle. A sum of money representing checks and other financial instruments that are outstanding in the process of delivery to the payee by the postal system or other carrier. Mail float covers the period of time beginning when the issuer releases the item to a carrier and ending when the item is delivered to the payee or its agent (e.g., its lockbox bank).

Negative Float: A sum of money representing Customer Float allocated in excess of actual Bank Float incurred on those customers' deposits. Negative Float represents monies received by the bank for deposited items that have not been made available to customers. Negative Float is generally considered a source of revenue for banks. Negative Float is also referred to as Reverse Float.

Noncheck Float: A sum of money representing financial instruments other than checks that are outstanding and in the process of collection.

Nonearning Assets: Assets that do not produce interest or other investment income. Nonearning Financial Assets are a subset of Nonearning Assets comprising such categories as Cash and Due From Accounts and Nonperforming Loans.

On-Us: Used to describe a check or other cash item drawn on your own financial institution.

Paying Bank: The bank on which a check or other financial instrument is drawn, and on which it must make payment when the item is presented.

Positive Float: A sum of money representing the difference between Bank Float and Customer

Float when a bank incurs more float on customers' deposits than it allocates as Customer Float. Positive Float represents monies that have been made available to depositing customers but that have not been collected by the Bank. Positive Float is generally considered a reduction of revenue for banks.

Presentment: The delivery of checks to the Paying Bank for payment.

Priced Float: See Customer Float.

Processing Float: A component of the float cycle. A sum of money representing checks and other financial instruments in the float cycle while under the physical control of a participant in that cycle. For example, a check recipient can incur processing float while posting payments to accounts receivable, preparing bank deposits, or delivering deposits to a bank. A bank can incur processing float while encoding and sorting checks, handling rejected items, balancing and preparation of cash letters.

Proof of Deposit: The process of comparing the total dollar amount of items deposited to the deposit amount to ensure that each deposit is in balance.

Proof Encoding: A process for handling deposited checks that performs two functions, Proof of Deposit and Encoding, in the same operation. Operators using special machines encode the amount on each item in magnetic ink, while the machine totals debits and credits to ensure that deposits are in balance.

Receiving Float: A sum of money representing checks and other financial instruments received as payments or receipts that are in the process of collection and conversion to money.

Remittance Processing: See Lockbox.

Return on Assets (ROA): A measure of bank financial performance. Return on assets equals annulalized net income divided by average assets, expressed as a percentage, usually carried to two decimal points. If the year's net income was $12.5 million and assets averaged $1 billion, Return on Assets was 1.25 percent.

$$\frac{\$12.5 \text{ million net income}}{\$1 \text{ billion average assets}} \times 100$$

$$= 1.25 \text{ ROA}$$

Return on Equity (ROE): A measure of bank financial performance. Return on equity equals annualized net income divided by average shareholder equity, expressed as a percentage, usually carried out to two decimal places. If the year's net income was $12.5 million and shareholder equity averaged 75 million, Return on Equity was 16.67 percent.

$$\frac{\$12.5 \text{ million net income}}{\$75 \text{ million average equity}} \times 100$$

$$= 16.67 \text{ ROE}$$

Reverse Float: See Negative Float.

**Required
Reserves:**   Funds that financial institutions must by law maintain in vault cash or in Federal Reserve Bank accounts to ensure liquidity to pay depositors claims. Required Reserves are equal to a fraction of transaction account and certain other deposit liabilities. Required Reserve accounts at Federal Reserve Banks currently do not earn interest or credit toward priced Federal Reserve services, and they are therefore considered nonearning assets.

Routing Number: A nine-digit number identifying the paying bank for a check or other financial instrument. The routing number is printed in magnetic ink on the bottom of each check. The assignment of Routing Numbers is administered by the American Bankers Association. The first four digits identify the Federal Reserve District and check processing region of the paying bank, while the next four digits identify the financial institution. The ninth digit is a check digit for automated processing. The Routing Number is sometimes referred to as the Transit Number, the Routing and Transit Number, The Transit Routing Number, The R/T Number, the ABA number, or the FR/ABA Number.

Sendpoint: The Check Clearing Intermediary to which a Cash Letter is sent, or the Paying Bank location to which a Direct Presentment is delivered.

Transit Deadline: A deadline for the dispatch of cash letters to a Check Clearing Intermediary or Paying Bank.

Transit Item: A check or other cash item drawn on a financial instition other than your own. Also referred to as Not-On-Us.

Unallocated Float: Any Bank Float not allocated to customers or internal bank units.

Unbooked Float: A sum of money representing checks and other financial instruments received by a bank, individual, or corporation that are outstanding and in the process of collection, but that have not been recorded on the financial books of that entity.

Vault Cash Coin and currency held by a financial institution.

About the Author

This work's author, William Swords is Manager of Check Processing Services for First Interstate Bank of California. An Analysis of Float in the *Commercial Banking Industry* (Bank Administration Institute, 1982), written by Littlewood Shain & Company and Bank Administration Institute, provided the backdrop against which this book was created. William Swords has worked in bank operations and product management for over 15 years, and he spent 5 years as a bank consultant. Mr. Swords has been a frequent speaker at Bank Administration Institute's Check Processing and Float Conferences.